The Royle Family

The Royle Family

The Scripts: Series 1

Caroline Aherne, Craig Cash
and Henry Normal

GRANADA
MEDIA

First published in Great Britain in 1999
By Granada Media, an imprint of André Deutsch Ltd
in association with Granada Media Group
76 Dean Street
London W1V 5HA
www.vci.co.uk

A catalogue record for this book is available
from the British Library

ISBN 0 233 99721 0

Typeset by Derek Doyle & Associates, Liverpool
Printed and bound in the UK by
MPG Books Ltd, Bodmin, Cornwall

3 5 7 9 10 8 6 4 2

For our families, for their inspiration

Contents

Introduction

Thank you for buying this book of scripts. With *The Royle Family* we wanted to write something about life as we knew it – the families that we grew up in.

We drew inspiration from all our families and friends, and bits of all of them are present in each character. The cast we chose brought them to life even better than in our imaginations.

For us, *The Royle Family* was a labour of love, so we were thrilled when it seemed to connect with viewers too.

There is a page of thank yous at the back of this book, but here we would like to thank Andy Harries, our executive producer, for never giving up on us.

Love

Caroline and Craig

Ealing Studios, August 1999

Cast list

DENISE ROYLE	CAROLINE AHERNE
DAVE BEST	CRAIG CASH
TWIGGY	GEOFFREY HUGHES
BARBARA ROYLE (MAM)	SUE JOHNSTON
MARY CARROLL	DOREEN KEOGH
ANTONY ROYLE	RALF LITTLE
JOE CARROLL	PETER MARTIN
NORMA SPEAKMAN (NANA)	LIZ SMITH
CHERYL CARROLL	JESSICA STEVENSON
JIM ROYLE (DAD)	RICKY TOMLINSON

Episode 1

Scene 1

(DAD, MAM, DENISE, MARY, ANTONY)

IT IS HALF PAST SIX ON A FEBRUARY FRIDAY EVENING. A 26-YEAR-OLD WORKING-CLASS GIRL, <u>DENISE ROYLE</u>, IS SITTING WATCHING TV WITH HER MAM. HER DAD, <u>JIM ROYALE</u>, IN HIS SIXTIES, IS SITTING READING A PHONE BILL. ALL THREE SMOKE CONSTANTLY THROUGHOUT.

Dad: Ninety-eight quid . . . it's good to talk my arse . . . (READING PHONE BILL) 929 1246, whose number's that?

Mam: It's Mary.

Dad: Mary! You've been ringing Mary next door? If you shouted she could hear you.

Denise: She can hear *you*.

Mam: Give it a rest the pair of you.

Dad: Rest my arse . . . two pound fifty phoning next door . . . she's in and out all day like a bloody yoyo. (PAUSE) I'll put you a serving hatch in.

Denise: You're tight as a crab's arse you.

Dad: Crab's arse my arse. Two pound fifty . . . good job she's cured her stutter.

Denise: The phone's there to be used.

Dad: The phone's there for emergencies. How many times do you see me ringing anyone?

Denise: Who you gonna ring? You've got no mates.

Dad: Talk of the devil!

PAUSE DURING WHICH DENISE AND MAM GO BACK TO WATCHING TV. DAD CONTINUES READING HIS PHONE BILL. KNOCK AT THE DOOR.

Mary: (KNOCKS AND ENTERS. SHE IS THE ONLY ONE WHO DOESN'T USE THE BELL) Only me.

Mam: Come in, Mary.

Denise: Hey, Mary, is your Cheryl in?

Mary: Yes.

Denise: Ask her to bring us round the catalogue will you.

Mary: Yes I will. (TO MAM) I've just come to wish you all the best for your new career, Barbara.

Dad: Career my arse, she's going to work part-time in the bakery. Why don't you go home, she'll ring you, tell you all about it.

Mam: (IGNORING LAST COMMENT) I've had our Denise testing me on the price list. I've got it off by heart up to pastries. Go on test me, Mary.

Mary: Vanilla Slice?

Mam: Thirty-eight p.

Mary: I'll have two.

THEY BOTH LAUGH. DAD LOOKS DISGUSTED.

Mary: I'll pop in the baker's tomorrow, see how you're getting on. Mind you I'm expecting a big discount.

THEY ALL LAUGH.

Dad: How much is a cup of tea in your bakery?

Mam: They don't do tea.

Dad: Same as here then. No chance of drowning.

Mam: (TAKING THE HINT) Will you be stopping for a brew, Mary?

Mary: No. I've got a pile of ironing and it won't do itself will it?

MARY AND MUM LAUGH AGAIN AS MARY EXITS.

All: See ya.

PAUSE.

Mary: Bye.

Dad: She's hilarious, Mary. How does she come up with them.

Mam: Come on, Denise, test us some more.

Denise: Crusty cob.

Dad: Who's been ringing Aberdeen?

Mam: (IGNORING DAD) Fourteen p.

Denise: Meat and potato pie?

Mam: Sixty-seven p.

Denise: No.

Mam: Sixty-eight p.

Denise: No.

Mam: Sixty-nine p.

Denise: No.

Mam: Oh shite . . . (LOOKS AT PRICE LIST)

LAUGHS.

Denise: Hey Mam, do they do wedding cake?

Mam: Up, yeh I'll be able to get a discount.

Denise: How much would one cost?

Mam: About two hundred quid.

Dad: How much!

Mam: Two hundred quid.

Denise: How many tiers is that?

Dad: There'll be plenty of bloody tears if it costs two hundred quid. Is his dad paying owt towards this wedding lark?

Denise: Dad, he's on a disability allowance.

Dad: So he's paying bugger all and he'll get a better parking space.

ANTONY ENTERS.

Antony: Any tea going, Mam?

Mam: Your tea's in the oven, love.

Antony: (EXITING TO KITCHEN) What is it?

DAD ADJUSTS HIS CROTCH.

Mam: Egg and chips.

Dad: (CALLING AFTER HIM) Antony, who do you know in Aberdeen?

Antony: (OOV, SHOUTING) Ugh, Mam . . . they're all soggy.

Dad: (CALLING INTO OTHER ROOM) Get 'em ate. They all goes to make a turd.

Mam: You're all going to have to get used to making your own.

ANTONY RE-ENTERS ROOM.

Dad: Your mother's a career woman. (TO ANTONY) Which room are you in . . . this room or that?

Antony: This room.

Dad: So what's the light on in that room for?

ANTONY SWITCHES LIGHT OFF IN OTHER ROOM.

Dad: Who do you think I am, bloody Rockafella?

ANTONY SITS AND WATCHES TV WITH FOOD ON HIS LAP.

Antony: Is that Lesley Joseph? In't there nowt on the other side?

PAUSE.

Dad: She's got a mouth like a horse. She wants a good swipe of shite, her.

LONG PAUSE.

Denise: Mam, tell Antony to shut his gob when he's eating.

DOORBELL GOES.

Mam: Antony, shut your gob when you're eating.

Cheryl: Hiya!

Denise: (GETTING UP) That'll be Cheryl with the catalogue.

DENISE EXITS TO THE FRONT DOOR.

Dad: Where did your Aunty Vi move to?

Mam: Middleton.

Dad: Not Aberdeen?

Mam: Middleton.

PAUSE. DAD LOOKS AT TV IN DISGUST.

Dad: All right, crabby arse, all right. Where's the bloody remote off the television?

CUT TO:

Scene 2

<u>INT. NIGHT–KITCHEN</u>
(CHERYL, DENISE, ANTONY, MAM (OOV))

CHERYL AND DENISE ARE LOOKING AT A CATALOGUE.

Cheryl: Only five pound fifteen a week . . . for forty weeks . . . real leather.

Denise: That's nothing that . . . shall we get one. What you having brown or black?

Cheryl: Brown.

Denise: I'll have black then, we don't want to look the same. (BEAT) Ey, Cheryl . . . Close your eyes. (SHE FLICKS THROUGH PAGES) Right, give us your finger. Right, open them.

DENISE HAS PLACED CHERYL'S FINGER ON A PHOTO OF A MAN'S UNDERPANTS. CHERYL SCREAMS AND WITH-DRAWS FINGERS.

Cheryl: What're you like? (TURNING PAGE TO LYCRA) Actually I wouldn't mind one of them.

Denise: His is a weird shape. That's not normal is it?

Cheryl: What's Dave? Y-fronts or boxers?

Denise: Whatever he wears, they're always full of skiddies.

THEY BOTH LOOK AT A BUNCH OF CATALOGUES IN A PROLONGED SILENCE.

Can't believe it's only six weeks to the wedding.

DENISE GETS UP AND MOVES TO COOKER. SHE TURNS ON RING.

Cheryl: I know, there's so much to sort out isn't there . . . who's doing your perm?

Denise: Sandra Beswick . . . eh guess what she's calling herself now, she's gone mobile: Sandy Scissors. In't it crap.

BOTH LAUGH – TURN TO LIGHT FAG.

Cheryl: You know I don't know what I'm going to do with my hair for the wedding. I might have some streaks put in.

Denise: Let me look at you. You'd look absolutely gorgeous with streaks.

Cheryl: Do you think so?

Denise: Yeh.

Cheryl: I've got to lose two stone as well.

Denise: I have.

Cheryl: There's nowt on you, you're tiny.

Denise: You're joking, I'm like a bleeding sumo me . . . (GRAB-BING FLESH) And I've got an arseful of cellulite . . . (MOVES BACK) Mind you, Dave likes girls with a bit of meat on them. (SITS)

Cheryl: Sexist pig.

Denise: Yeh he is . . . ey, thank God.

THEY BOTH LAUGH.

Cheryl: Eh, is Gary from the butchers still Dave's best man?

Denise: Yeh . . .

Cheryl: He's gorgeous him.

Denise: Get out, he stinks of mince.

Cheryl: I'd shag him.

Denise: Yeh, I would.

ANTONY ENTERS WITH EMPTY PLATE.

Mam (OOV): (SHOUTS FROM THE LIVING ROOM) Pour the tea Antony.

Antony: Tut, they waited for me to come in here.

GETS THREE MUGS OUT AND PUTS MILK AND PLENTY OF SUGARS IN, THEN POURS TEA DURING DIALOGUE BELOW.

Cheryl: Hiya, Antony.

Denise: He's having to wear a suit.

Cheryl: Have you got a girlfriend yet?

Denise: Yes, his hand. (BOTH GIRLS LAUGH) Here Cheryl, that'd look good on you.

Antony: What is it, a tent?

Denise: Antony . . . keep that (POINTING TO HER NOSE) out, that (POINTING TO HER MOUTH) shut or you'll get them (EYES) blacked.

Cheryl: Cheeky get.

ANTONY CROSSES WITH MUGS.

Denise: Hey. (MEANING TEAS) Where's ours?

Antony: (LEAVING ROOM) Kiss it.

Denise: (SHOUTING) Mam, Antony's being cheeky to Cheryl. (MOVING TO TEAPOT) I'll make ours, he don't wash his hands.

CUT TO:

Scene 3

INT. NIGHT–LIVING ROOM
(MAM, DAD, DAVE)

ANTONY ENTERS WITH TEAS. DAD IS LOOKING ROUND FOR THE REMOTE. ENTER DAVE FROM OUTSIDE DOOR.

Dad: Get that will you, Antony.

Antony: It's only Dave.

Mam: Hiya Dave love. Are you all right?

Dave: Yeh, smashing. Hi Jim. Is there owt on?

Mam: It's only *Home and Away*. Have you had your tea, Dave?

Dave: Yeh.

Mam: What did you have?

Dave: Cornbeef hash.

Mam: We should have that one night. (TO DAD) Jim, Dave's had cornbeef hash.

Dad: Funny it never mentioned it on the news.

Dave: All right, Jim?

Dad: Oh aye, can't smile wide enough me.

Dave: She in there?

Mam: Yeh.

Dad: Dave . . . how's your mate in Aberdeen?

Dave: I haven't got a mate in Aberdeen.

Dad: Just checking.

Mam: (TO DAVE) Ignore him.

DAVE EXITS.

CUT TO:

Scene 4

INT. NIGHT–KITCHEN
(DAVE, DENISE, CHERYL, MAM (OOV), TWIGGY (OOV)

DAVE ENTERS.

Dave: (TO DENISE) Hey you . . . don't be thinking of buying owt in there.

Denise: I'm not. (EXCHANGES LOOK WITH CHERYL) Cheryl's just been looking at men's nobs.

Dave: No change there then. You two all right for a brew. Gary was asking after you Cheryl

Cheryl: Uh yeh, what did he say?

Dave: He wanted to know if you're a goer?

Denise: What did you say?

Dave: I said you go like the clappers.

Cheryl: In his dreams. He changes his clothes less than Noddy him.

Denise: Have you had your tea?

Dave: Yeh.

Cheryl: What did you have?

Dave: Cornbeef hash.

Denise: Did ya? Did you get that wedding car sorted?

Dave: I've not had time to wipe mi'arse.

Denise: I know, I've seen your undies.

Dave: Ho, ho.

Denise: Better get it sorted, I'm not going in that poxy transit.

Dave: It was all right for you Tuesday night

Denise: (LAYING DOWN THE LAW) Hey! Cheryl don't want to hear it, all right.

Cheryl: I do.

Dave: She does.

Denise: She don't.

PAUSE.

Cheryl: So, who's doing your disco at the wedding?

Dave: Me.

Denise: You can't do it, you're the bleedin' groom.

Dave: All right Gary can do the first hour. Get it going.

Denise: Bring Gary on honeymoon, he can do the first hour there, get me going.

BOTH GIRLS LAUGH.

Dave: Oh, did I tell you I'm getting a load of professional business cards done . . . from this place in Knutsford.

Denise: Oh, Knutsford's well posh.

Dave: Yeh, Knutsford Service Station . . . three quid for fifty. The first gig you get from them they pay for themselves don't they? . . . You know, you just put price up by three quid . . . and after that, it's clear profit in't it?

Denise: Good idea.

Dave: That's me kiddo.

Cheryl: What you having wrote on it?

Dave: 'You've heard the rest. Now here's the best . . . Dave Best . . . Mobile Disco'.

Denise: Where's my name? You should put 'Dave and Denise'; I've been to all your gigs.

Dave: So's my mam and dad . . . do you want their name on it an'all?

Denise: Ey and you're not just having them cards to try and pull the birds.

Dave: Give it a rest.

WE HEAR THE DOORBELL FAINTLY.

Denise: Well have my name put on it an'll then.

Dave: What – and let all the women know I'm taken.

Denise: Cheeky get!

CUT TO:

Scene 5

INT. NIGHT–LIVING ROOM
(DAVE, DENISE, CHERYL, TWIGGY, ANTONY, DAD, MAM)

DAVE ENTERS, FOLLOWED BY DENISE AND CHERYL WITH GREETINGS FOR TWIGGY. TWIGGY IS A LARGE SCALLY BLOKE.

Antony: It's all right, it's only Twiggy.

Dad: (TO KITCHEN) Eh, Twiggy's here.

Mam: Hiya Twiggy, all right. (TO TWIGGY) How's your mam's legs love?

Twiggy: Still under the hospital.

Mam: Tell her I was asking for her.

All: Hiya Twiggy.

Twiggy: Right . . . Now. How you fixed for denim . . . feel the quality of that.

Dad: You've not got any wedding dresses in there?

Twiggy: No . . . these are jeans.

Denise: What make are they?

Twiggy: Top gear . . . quality stuff . . . tenner a pair.

Cheryl: Got owt for me?

Antony: Yeh . . . the one's he's wearing.

Mam: Eh Jim, why don't you get a pair? Them pants have gone at the crotch.

Dad: Don't look then.

Denise: Go on Dad, try some on.

Dad: I don't wear jeans.

Dave: Go on, Jim . . . everybody wears them nowadays.

Twiggy: Come on . . . pants'll cost you three times the price of these and these'll last you twice as long. Try them on.

Dad: Give us a pair here. (HE EXITS)

Twiggy: What about you, Denise?

Denise: I've not got the arse for jeans.

Twiggy: You have, you've got a gorgeous arse you have . . . you'll find these out a treat.

Dave: Hey! That's my fiancé's arse you're talking about.

Twiggy: Yeh . . . and that's your arse you're talking through. (TO MAM) I'll tell you what, I've got a load of Wash'n'Go, I don't know whether you're interested.

Mam: What've you got?

Twiggy: Wash'n'Go, y'know the stuff that bird in the ad washes with and pisses off. It's the genuine stuff but with Arabic writing on it. Fifty p a bottle

RESPONSE FROM OTHERS.

Please yourself.

Cheryl: Go on then Twiggy, I'll have two quid's worth.

Twiggy: Tell you what . . . for you luv, cos you're my best-looking customer . . . I'll throw in a box of panty pads. Now how are you for jeans Cheryl?

Cheryl: I'm on a diet. I don't really know what size to get.

Twiggy: Well . . . if they're too tight I'll help you out of em.

NUDGING MAM, BOTH LAUGH.

Mam: Uh, Twiggy, you're a right cheeky beggar. Ahh, how's little Lee?

Twiggy: She lets me see him every other Saturday and every third Wednesday from four till seven.

Mam: He must be getting big now.

Twiggy: Yeh, he's twelve in August. I'll tell you what, he's a fussy little bleeder . . . it's got to be Nike this and Levi that . . . he won't touch any of this shite . . . So what you doing Cheryl . . . are you having a pair or what?

Cheryl: No. I don't think so.

DAD RETURNS IN JEANS. ALL LAUGH EXCEPT DAD.

Dad: All right you shower of shite.

Dave: Hey, it's John Wayne.

Twiggy: Here give em back . . . you'll give me a bad name.

Dad: Laugh all you want, I'm keeping these. My money's in my other trousers. I owe you a tenner, Twiggy. It's like ruddy Blackpool illuminations in here . . . turn that lamp off. Turn that fire off an'all. If you're cold get a vest on. Where's the remote Barbara?

Mam: It's on top of the telly.

Dad: What good's it there? Antony, chuck it over you lazy little sod.

Twiggy: Now listen, is anyone else buying?

Mam: Antony?

Antony: Not if he's wearing some . . . no way.

PAUSE.

Denise: Hey, Twiggy . . . next time you're in the baker's guess who'll serve you?

Twiggy: Who?

Denise: My mam.

Mam: Me.

Twiggy: Is that right, Barbara? I'm always in there.

Mam: What do you have?

Twiggy: Two cornish pasties, a sausage roll and a cream Danish.

Mam: One pound thirty-two. Am I right?

Twiggy: I haven't a clue. I'll see you in there tomorrow. (HE STANDS) I'll drop you that shampoo off on Saturday.

All: (AS TWIGGY EXITS) See ya.

Dad: He's a scruffy get that Twiggy. Wouldn't you think he'd do something about his weight.

PAUSE.

Mam: How's your diet going, Cheryl?

Cheryl: Really good, I've stuck to it for a fortnight now.

Mam: Have you lost owt?

Cheryl: No. Right, well I'm off then.

CHERYL CROSSES BEHIND SOFA. DAVE TAKES HER SEAT.

Denise: Tra Cheryl.

Mam: Bye Cheryl. (PAUSE) Have you asked her to be bridesmaid?

Denise: Yeh, she's thrilled.

Dad: Bridesmaid my arse. She'll look like a bloody Easter egg on legs.

Antony: You're only having her as a bridesmaid to make you look better.

Denise: Get lost, Antony.

Mam: Is she really on a diet?

Denise: Yeh.

Mam: Do you think she'll ever get married?

Antony: Who'd have her?

Dad: Stevie Wonder. (PAUSE. REACTING TO CHRIS EVANS ON TV) Oh hell, it's him again . . . he's all about like shit in a field.

Denise: Leave it on Dad.

Dad: (REACTING TO TV) She's had a face-lift. They all have.

Denise: Shut it Dad we're missing it.

PAUSE. WE HEAR CHRIS EVANS ON TV.

Dad: Look at that gobshite . . . full of himself. He's like my arse, best kept out of sight.

Denise: He's a millionaire him, Dad.

Dad: He's still got ginger bollocks.

Mam: That reminds me I've got some tangerines in the kitchen. Who wants a tangerine?

Dad: (LOOKING DISGUSTED) How does your mind work, Barbara?

Denise: Are you nervous about tomorrow, Mam?

Mam: Yeh I won't sleep a wink.

Dad: What the hell is there to be nervous about – there's only your mates going in by the sound of it.

MAM REACTS. PAUSE.

Dave: Did I tell you I saw Duckers down the Chinese?

Denise: Terry Duckers?

Dave: Yeh.

Mam: Is he out?

Dad: No, they've got a Chinese in the nick.

Dave: He'd just got out, Barbara.

Mam: What's his missus say?

Dave: He'd not been home, yet.

Dad: What was he in for?

Dave: Beef Satay, half rice, half chips.

ALL BUT DAD LAUGH.

Dad: What was he in for, nobhead?

Dave: I know . . . He was in for receiving wasn't he?

Denise: Wasn't jeans was it?

PAUSE.

Mam: We should have Beef Satay one night.

Mam: (FINDING NO FAGS IN HER PACKET) Hey our Antony, nip down to the offie and get us some ciggies.

Antony: Ahh, Mam.

Dave: I'll go.

Denise: No, you sit there, let him go.

Mam: (GIVING ANTONY MONEY) Twenty for me and twenty for your Dad. What about you Denise?

Denise: Yeh, get us twenty.

MAM SITS.

Antony: (STANDING) Any advance on sixty?

Denise: I hate it when you eat them scratchings, Dad.

Antony: Can I get ten for myself out of the change?

Mam: You know what I've told you about smoking. You're only fifteen, you can't smoke until you're old enough to buy your own.

ANTONY TUTS AND LEAVES.

Mam: Don't slam that . . . door.

DOOR SLAMS – MAM REACTS.

Denise: (TO DAD) Do you know what's in them pork scratchings, Dad?

Dad: No.

Denise: Eyeholes, earholes and arseholes.

Dad: That's rissoles.

Denise: Oh, yes.

PAUSE.

Mam: Who keeps leaving mugs down on this coffee-table with no coasters?

Denise/Dad: (TOGETHER) Antony.

PAUSE.

Dave: I told Duckers he could come to the wedding.

Denise: You didn't.

Dave: I did.

Denise: You better be winding me up.

Dave: No, I told him.

Denise: What did you invite him for? He's a right nobhead. Tell you what, if he's going I'm not.

DAVE MIMICS REELING IN A FISH.

Dave: Reel her in. One–nil.

ALL BUT DENISE LAUGH.

Denise: You're hilarious you, Dave.

Dave: Did I ever tell you what a lovely daughter you've got, James?

Dad: Yeh, last time you got the wrong side of her.

Dave: I wouldn't invite Terry Duckers y'lemon. Come 'ere . . . give us a kiss.

Denise: Kiss me arse.

Dave: I would do, I've had nowt all day . . .

Denise: You're having nowt all night . . .

Dave: I'nt she lovely Barbara . . . ? Eh, you know what they say, if you want to know what your wife'll look like when she's older, just look at the mother.

Dad: Hey, you're not calling the wedding off at this late stage.

Dave: No, that's meant as a compliment, Barbara.

Mam: Thanks, Dave love, at least someone appreciates me round here.

Dad: What's he after?

Denise: Ah, Dave . . . I'll make it up with you if you massage my feet.

DAVE RUBS DENISE'S FEET.

Mam: Do you know, you've got lovely feet, our Denise. You've got the nicest feet in our family, Denise. (TAKING OFF SLIP-PERS) Look at mine, Dave . . . they're buggered.

Dad: Look at this dopey sod . . . she's got him right where she wants him . . . he's been at work all day . . . she's sat on her big fat arse . . . and he's massaging her feet. I don't know what the world's coming to.

Mam: Why don't you ever rub my feet?

Dad: What them bloody trotters? I'd need asbestos gloves and a gas mask.

MAM INSPECTS HER FEET.

Mam: Eh, I think I've got a verruca coming.

Denise: Oh, yeh?

ANTONY RETURNS AND GIVES MUM FAGS AND CHANGE.

Antony: Here y'are, Mam.

Mam: (TO ANTONY) Thanks love. Hey young man, what have I told you about leaving mugs on the coffee-table without using a coaster.

Dad: Have you got a gig tonight, Dave?

Dave: I'm on down the Feathers. It's Tony Macca's sister's eighteenth.

Denise: What, Beverly Macca from the Co-op?

Dave: Yeh.

Mam: Is she eighteen now? Are her kids going?

Dave: Yeh.

Mam: Who's the father of them two?

Dave: Don't know.

Denise: Could be anyone's in the Feathers.

Antony: Could by anyone's in trousers.

Denise: You fancy her. She's a right slapper.

Mam: Ah, I always feel a bit sorry for her with them two kids. She has it hard.

Denise: She likes it hard, that's her trouble.

PAUSE.

Dad: How much is a pint in there now?

Denise: Oh Dave, have you farted?

Dave: What?

Dave: No, that's one of your dad's.

Dad: He who smelt it, dealt it.

Antony: It smells like cornbeef that.

Mam: We're going to have that one day.

DAD GIVES MAM A DESPAIRING LOOK.

Hey I've just thought . . . who's going to make tea tomorrow, I'll be working?

Dad: You're all right love, we'll wait till you get back.

Mam: Why does everything in this house have to revolve around me?

PAUSE.

Dad: This bakery job's more trouble than it's worth.

DAVE FARTS AGAIN.

Denise: It was you.

DAVE REACTS.

Dad: See, it weren't me.

Mam: (TO DAVE) You dirty article.

Dad: In Middle Eastern countries that's a sign of respect.

Denise: That's burping!

Dad: Same difference. Different hole.

Dave: (TO DENISE) You fart, Denise.

Denise: I do not.

Antony: She does, I've smelt it.

Denise: Antony, my mam told me not to tell you this but you were adopted.

Antony: (STICKING TWO FINGERS UP) Are these yours Denise?

PHONE RINGS.

Denise/Mam: Get that, Antony.

ANTONY GOES TO ANSWER IT.

Dad: If that's the Invisible Man tell him I can't see him.

Antony: (ANSWERING PHONE) Hello. Hiya Nana. Do you want m'mam?

Mam: (TO ANTONY) Can't you have a bit of conversation with her. She's on her own all day.

Antony: Aint got nowt to say to her.

Mam: Well make something up. Hiya Mam . . . have you had your tea? Yeh . . . What did you have. We've had that . . . Dave's had cornbeef hash.

Dad: Who's she on to, Lloyd Grossman?

Mam: Oh it's all go here . . . we're up to our eyes in it. I can't seem to get nowt done. It's all go . . . yeh. What date was on the voucher? The miserable sod. Do you want to talk to Jim?

MAN THROWS PHONE TO DAD

Dad: (DOWN PHONE. BRIGHT AND CHEERFUL) Hiya Norma love . . . how are you doing? (INTERRUPTING AS BEST HE CAN) Hang on a minute our Denise wants a word with you. She won't let me speak to you. (THROWS PHONE TO DENISE).

Denise: Hiya Nana, are you all right? Yeh . . . yeh . . .

DENISE CONTINUES TO LISTEN TO NANA'S STORY ON THE PHONE IN THE BACKGROUND AD LIBBING THE OCCASIONAL WORD.

Mam: (TO DAD) It's shocking really . . . she's eighty-two.

Dad: Why what's happened?

Mam: She took a voucher in the shop and it was a day out of date and the manager wouldn't let her have the money off.

Dad: How much was this voucher worth?

Mam: Twenty p.

Dad: Twenty p? It'll cost her more than that to ring every bugger she knows and his dog to tell them.

Denise: Well if they're too tight, take one of the insoles out. All right, I'll give you back to Mam . . . see you Nana.

Mam: Yeh . . . I told Jim. He was livid with them.

DAD REACTION.

These things are sent to try us . . . yeh. Bye Mam . . . chin up. (SHE PUTS THE PHONE OFF.) She's getting worse i'nt she – bless her. Here, put that back.

ANTONY RETURNS PHONE TO HALL.

Antony: I'm going to Darren's.

All: See ya.

DOOR SLAMS – MAM REACTS.

Dave: We'd best be off and all.

Denise: Just let me put some tutty on.

DENISE STARTS TO PUT MAKE-UP ON.

Mam: Eh Denise, give us a god of that new lippy, our Denise. It's a lovely colour in't it. I can't usually wear red. It does nothing for me. I can't wear red can I Jim?

Dad: No, that's what's held you back all these years.

Mam: (LOOKING IN MIRROR) Do you know I am looking my age. Just this last few months it's crept up on me. Mind you, it could be worse, at least I've still got my schoolgirl figure.

Dad: I must clean that mirror.

Denise: Get lost, Dad. Mam's got a great figure for a woman her age.

Mam: It's going to be so tempting working at that baker's. I don't want to put on any weight before the wedding. I want to get myself a nice suit.

Dad: Go in your school uniform, it still fits you du'n't it?

Denise: What you wearing, Dad.?

Dad: A bloody big hole in mi' pocket be looks of it.

Mam: (IGNORING DAD) Hey Dave, has your mam got her outfit for the wedding?

Dave: No, not yet, she's getting a suit from Marks.

Mam: Uh Dave, you best find out which one it is. I'd hate to get one the same, it would be awful.

Denise: Come on, let's go and see Beverly yoyo nickers then. See you late, Mam. Be in about one o'clock.

Mam: All right love.

Dave: See y'.

Denise: Hey Dad, if my mate Angus from Aberdeen rings tell him . . . (AS DAD REACTS) Ah, I'm only joking.

Dad: See y'buggerlugs.

DENISE AND DAVE EXIT.
PAUSE.

Mam: Do you hear that, Jim: Marks's, Dave's Mam, hey?

Dad: Never mind, you'd look better than her in an old sack.

Mam: Might have to. (GETTING UP) I'm going to have a bath. Is the immersion on?

Dad: I expect so, everything else is.

Mam: Do you want to get in after me?

Dad: Aye, go on.

MAM EXITS LEAVING ROOM EMPTY BUT FOR DAD. PAUSE.
DAD GETS UP AND ADMIRES HIS ARSE THEN DOES
COWBOY DRAW IN MIRROR.

END OF EPISODE.

Episode 2

Scene 1

<u>INT. TEATIME–LIVING ROOM</u>
(DAD, MAM, DENISE, MARY, ANTONY)

DAD AND DENISE ARE AT THE TABLE WHICH IS SET FOR
FOUR. THE TV IS ON LOW THROUGHOUT. MAM ENTERS
WITH TWO PLATES OF FOOD.

Dad: Where's mine, Barb?

Mam: It's coming, I've only got one pair of hands. Do you know
him from the flats?

Dad: Who? There's loads of people in the flats.

Mam: (SITTING AT TABLE) You know which one . . . he used
to have a string for a belt.

Dad: Him . . . bloody Worzel Gummage, too tight to buy a belt
but he could always afford a bloody pint.

Mam: He came in the baker's today.

Dad: And?

Mam: He bought a sliced loaf.

Dad: What did you tell me that for?

Mam: You can't say anything in this house without having your head bitten off by that nowty sod.

PAUSE. EVERYONE EATS.

Denise: We should go on *Family Fortunes* one time.

Mam: Oh no, I'd go to pieces.

Dad: What! Most of these families are thick as pigshit. Les Dennis is no bloody better, if you put his brains in a bloody hazelnut they'd still rattle. Hey, remember that time when they said they'd asked a hundred people to name something green . . . and the old woman who was the contestant said her cardigan.

Antony: (IMMITATING 'WRONG' NOISE FROM PROGRAMME) Uh-er . . .

Mam: What's wrong with that . . . it was green?

Dad: How would the bloody members of the public know – they'd never seen her. Don't bother writing, Denise, your mother, she'd make a show of us. (TO DENISE) What's up with you . . . you've got a face like a slapped arse?

Denise: I didn't want beans.

Mam: There's hardly any there.

Antony: I'll have them.

Denise: I didn't want them touching the chop.

Dad: Who do you think you are, Lady Muck?

Denise: I've got bean juice on my chop now. You've got bean juice on your beard.

Dad: I was saving that for after.

Mam: Mary next door's got a microwave.

Denise: Me and Dave's going to have a microwave . . . do you think I should get a food processor?

Dad: What for? Just stick to the chip pan love.

Denise: We're not going to have chips every night.

Mam: What are you going to have then?

Denise: I don't know, we might have pasta and stuff like that.

Dad: Pasta my arse.

Mam: Have you told Dave this?

Denise: Yeh.

Dad: And he still wants to marry you?

Denise: He's not marrying me for what I'm like in the kitchen.

Antony: It's what you're like in the bedroom.

Dad: Hey, cut it out.

Denise: (TO ANTONY) Who threw you nuts? (TO MAM) What I'm going to do is . . . I'm going to make lasagne and I'm going to stick it in the freezer so he can heat it up when he gets home.

Mam: Look at you Denise . . . you've got it all mapped out. I wish I was like you. You know, when I was your age we knew nothing.

Denise: It's only stuff we've read in magazines.

Antony: So who's getting you a freezer?

Denise: I don't know yet . . . it's on the wedding list . . . with the microwave and I'm going to put a food processor on it.

Dad: Is there owt cheaper on this wedding list?

Denise: I'm gonna get a dishwasher an'all. I've told Dave. If he thinks I'm washing pots every night he's got another thing coming. They're going right in that dishwasher.

Dad: Are you gonna eat the fat on your chop?

Denise: No . . .

Dad: Give it here.

PAUSE.

Mam: I'll go to that butcher's again.

Denise: That's the one where Dave's mate Gary works.

Antony: Him who smells of mince?

Denise: That's him. You should have got him to serve you. He'd have given you a bit extra.

Mam: He was out the back mincing.

Denise: I hope he's not going to come round all the time when we're married. He's a right nobhead him. I wish he'd just get himself a girlfriend.

Mam: Didn't he go out with that Sandra Beswick at one time?

Denise: She couldn't stand him. He had all blood under his fingernails. Did I tell you she's gone mobile now?

Mam: Who Sandra Beswick?

Denise: Calling herself Sandy Scissors now but I'm still calling her Sandra.

Mam: Everyone's going mobile nowadays.

Denise: She only needs to do four clients a day to cover costs she reckons.

Mam: So how many does she do?

Denise: About seven a day.

Dad: She must be raking it in.

Mam: How much does she charge for a perm?

Denise: Well, only twenty-two quid but don't forget she's using all your electricity and water . . . supping your brews.

Mam: It's a dear do that. I don't think I could afford to have myself done mobile.

Dad: You should have got yourself a trade like hairdressing, Denise.

Denise: I don't want to go round doing scabby old women's hair. Our Antony should be the one hairdressing the amount of time he spends on his own.

Antony: As if.

Denise: Dave goes to Uni-cut.

Antony: He's only weighing up the talent.

Denise: What do you mean?

Antony: Loads of dolly-birds in there.

Denise: Get lost, I wouldn't be marrying him if he were like that.

Mam: All men are like that.

Denise: He don't look at other girls when I'm with him.

Mam: Don't he?

Denise: No, I'd knock his bloody block off.

PAUSE.

Mam: When you're married what night will you and Dave be coming round for your tea?

Dad: It's took us twenty-six years to get rid of her.

Denise: I think we'll come round Tuesdays and Thursdays. I'll have to check with Dave though.

Mam: I'll do some of that pasta stuff if that's what you want.

Dad: Pasta my arse.

Denise: We'll have to go round his mam and dad's one night.

Dad: You want to pack sandwiches then. Has his dad ever worked or has he always been on this disability lark?

Denise: Yeh . . . I think he worked at Duggans.

Dad: That closed twelve years ago. Can he get me on that disability allowance?

Denise: He's got a bone disease.

Dad: Aye, bone idleness.

Denise: Dad, will you give over.

Dad: I've got to sweat blood to pay for this wedding of yours and that lazy sod's paying bugger-all.

Mam: It's always money with you, isn't it Jim?

Denise: Hey Dad, why don't you not bother making a speech at the wedding, just copy a list of the costs and hand it round.

Dad: I'd give a copy to Peg-leg for a start.

Denise: Put another record on, Dad.

Dad: It'd be a record if he bought a drink.

Mam: How are you getting on with Dave?

Denise: Fine.

Mam: Ah, he'll be having his tea now won't he?

Denise: Yeh.

Mam: Ah, he's a lovely lad.

Dad: You could've done worse. You could've married his father.

Denise: There's absolutely nothing left on that chop.

Mam: Have you finished, Antony?

Dad: Take it off him before he wipes the pattern off it.

Mam: (TAKING PLATES AWAY) Who wants apple pie?

Antony: Yeh.

Dad: Did you make it, love?

Mam: No.

Dad: Go on, I'll have some then.

Mam: Cheeky so-and-so.

Denise: I'll have some.

Dad: Keep hers away from the beans.

MAM EXITS.

Antony: Dad, can you do us a borrow?

Dad: Borrow my arse. Tell you what, I should be entitled to disability allowance, this wedding's bloody crippling me.

Denise: Do you know what gets me, right . . . on the night you'll be getting everyone drinks, showing off, like you're Mr Generoushead.

Dad: I can't do right for doing wrong me.

PAUSE.

Mam: (RETURNING WITH PIE FOR DAD AND ANTONY) I feel bad not being able to dance with him.

Dad: Who?

Mam: Dave's dad.

PAUSE WHILST MAM EXITS AGAIN AND RE-ENTERS WITH TWO MORE.

Antony: I love squirty cream.

Mam: Oh, I've got to go to Marks's tomorrow to get Mary next door a long cardigan.

Dad: Why are you buying Mary clothes?

Mam: It's a birthday present from Joe.

Dad: What are you doing buying Joe's presents?

Mam: He don't know what she wants.

Dad: How do you know she wants a cardi?

Mam: I asked her.

Dad: Why don't he ask her?

Mam: It's a surprise. Besides, I can't see Joe in Marks's can you?

Dad: Make sure he pays you for it.

Denise: What are you getting her, Mam?

Mam: I'll give her that bubble-bath I got from Aunty Margaret.

Antony: Any more of that pie, Mam, it's beautiful?

Mam: No, you've had the lot.

Dad: Have you got worms?

MAM, DAD AND DENISE ALL LIGHT UP.

Antony: Giz one, Mam.

Dad: You shouldn't be smoking. It's bad for you.

Antony: I only want one.

Mam: Are you getting them pots washed?

Antony: Ah it's Denise's turn . . . oh all right.

Mam: Go on, take one.

ANTONY TAKES ONE AND EXITS.

Dad: You shouldn't bribe him, he lives here rent free.

Mam: They're dead strict about no smoking in the baker's. No ways can you light up. It's health and safety. We have to keep taking it in turns to nip to the toilet.

Dad: You can't do owt these days. Them health and safety won't let you wipe your arse.

Mam: Some places are only taking on non-smokers.

Denise: Well, you just don't smoke in the interview do you.

Dad: What places?

Mam: Well flat-nosed Alan went for a job at the petrol station on the roundabout.

DAD GOES AND SITS IN HIS FAVOURITE CHAIR. PAUSE.

Dad: (REACTING TO TV) She's a big girl that Vanessa.

Mam: Tell me if I get like that won't you.

PAUSE.

Were you and Dave arguing last night?

Denise: He was doing my head it. He won't talk proper about the wedding.

Dad: What's there to talk about? I'm paying for it and his dad's paying nowt.

PAUSE. DAD DOES BIG BURP. DENISE GIVES HIM DISGUSTED LOOK. PAUSE.

Dad: Are you gonna make a brew or what? I've got a throat like Gandhi's flip-flop.

Mam: Let me finish me ciggi. (SHORT PAUSE. TO DENISE) How did you leave it with Dave?

Denise: I was telling him what we wanted for the wedding and he's more interested in his kebab and watching telly.

Mam: I wanted to come down and see what was happening but he (DAD) wouldn't let me.

Denise: He'd have liked to go abroad like Karen and Gareth. Did I tell you? They got married in the Seychelles. Had the ceremony on the beach.

Mam: Uh, I wouldn't like that. That's selfish. It's a day for your family.

Antony: Pamela Anderson got married in a white bikini!

Denise: What's that got to do with it?

Antony: I'm just telling you.

Dad: He wouldn't have too much to take off on her wedding night.

Denise: Not as if he hadn't seen it all before, we all have.

Antony: Hey Dad, would you?

Dad: What?

Antony: Pamela Anderson?

Dad: Would I? . . . No . . . I got everything I want in your mother. (TO MAM) Are you making a brew or not?

MAM GOES TO MAKE TEA. DENISE PICKS UP NEWSPAPER AND STARTS TO FLICK THROUGH. PAUSE.

Antony: Dad, how come Charlie Liddle from the Feathers always wears a suit?

Dad: I don't know, some men do, 'specially older men.

Antony: What do you mean?

Dad: Your grandad was same, my dad. He always wore a suit, shirt and tie.

Antony: How come you don't then?

Dad: I'm with it, me.

PAUSE. MAM BRINGS IN TEA.

Denise: Mam, will you tell Antony to stop slurping his tea:

Mam: Antony, stop slurping your tea.

Antony: Dave eats like a pig and you never say owt to him.

Denise: He doesn't eat like a pig. That's asthma thanks very much.

Dad: The two of you could eat for bloody England, the pair of you.

Denise: Dad, stop fiddling with yourself.

Dad: I'm not fiddling with myself . . . I paid a quid for these underpants. I've got fifty pence worth stuck up my arse.

Denise: Mam tell him.

Mam: She's right, if you're not picking your arse, you're picking your teeth.

Dad: I'll pick what I want in my own house. When you get your own house Denise you can pick what you want . . . your nose, your arse, your teeth, treat yourself.

Mam: I'm ashamed of this family, I really am.

PAUSE.

You know that Donna who works with me. She only does half days, afternoons and her mam usually picks up the kids. But the thing is her mam's going into hospital, means she won't be able to pick the kids up. So Donna wanted to swop to mornings. So she had to ask Pauline and she said 'Can I swop to mornings' and she told her about her mam and the hospital but Pauline was having none of it. She's got herself in a right pickle. So what's she going to do?

Denise: Who are you on about?

Mam: Donna.

Dad: What's the matter with her?

Mam: Her mam – usually picks the kids up from school but she can't because she's going into hospital and Pauline won't let Donna switch to mornings so she's stuck for someone to pick the kids up.

Dad: What's that got to do with you? It's not your problem.

Mam: I'm just telling you.

Dad: Don't you think I've got enough to worry about myself.

Mam: You've got no interest in anyone else but yourself, Jim.

PAUSE.

(TO DENISE) Oh your nana's coming for the day, Sunday.

Denise: Who's going to pick her up?

Mam: Your dad can go and get her on the bus.

Dad: Why can't she get the bus on her own?

Mam: She's eighty-two.

Dad: She should know the way then.

Mam: You're going.

Dad: She manages to get the bus to bingo every week.

Mam: You'd go if it were your mother.

Dad: I'd have a job, she's been dead fifteen years.

Mam: Ah. She'll be looking forward to coming all week.

Antony: All she does when she comes here is watch telly.

Mam: Well it's nice for her to watch telly in someone else's home. It's company for her.

Dad: If I get like that, shoot me.

Antony: Who's got a gun?

Dad: Hey mallethead, have you done them pots yet?

Mam: (TO DENISE) She was asking what you wanted for your wedding. I said you were best off with the money. So she's putting you a fiver in an envelope.

Denise: Ah, bless her.

Dad: Bless her my arse, it's five pound fifty a head for the meal. She's fifty p up before she gets there.

PAUSE.

What time does she want me to go for her?

Mam: Make it half eleven so she's got plenty of time to get herself sorted in the morning.

Dad: What, find her teeth you mean?

Mam: I think I'll do chicken.

Antony: Bagsey me breast.

Dad: Is there any tea left, berk?

Mam: Oh Jim, it's be stewed by now.

Dad: As long as it's wet and warm. Action man, do the honours. What's on tonight?

PAUSE AS HE READS.

I'm bloody sick of *Colombo*.

Mam: Who's that one in the wheelchair?

Dad: Dave's dad.

Denise: *Ironside* actually I think you'll find, Dad.

Mam: I saw him in another thing walking once.

Dad: Well it wasn't *Ironside* then was it?

Mam: No, but it was him.

Dad: What was his name? (REMEMBERING) Raymond Burr, I'll never forget his name as long as I live.

Denise: You just did.

DAD AND DENISE GIVE EACH OTHER A LOOK.

Dad: He only did two series of *Ironside*. He got sick of being pushed around. I wonder if he got disability allowance?

Mam: Don't start.

PAUSE. ANTONY PICKS UP DAD'S NEWSPAPER.

Dad: Do you know old Frank, goes in the Feathers, sits in the corner under the dartboard, he's the spit of Carl Maulden from *The Streets of San Francisco*. Looks like he's got an arse on the end of his nose.

THEY ALL LAUGH.

Mam: Ah, he's had a hard life, old Frank.

Dad: He's not making it any easier sitting under that dartboard.

Mam: He's a stubborn old bugger. He always says he was there long before that dartboard.

Denise: I saw him yesterday.

Dad: Where was he, in the eye hospital?

Denise: No. He was asleep in the bus shelter.

Mam: Poor Frank.

DOORBELL GOES.

Denise: Get that, Antony.

Antony: I have to do everything round here.

Dad: It might be bloody Snow White lookin' for you.

DOOR OPENS AND DAVE WALKS IN.

Antony: It's all right it's only Dave.

Dave: Hiya.

Denise: Hiya.

Mam: Hiya Dave, love . . . are you all right?

Dave: Yeh. Smashin' Barbara.

Mam: Have you had your tea, Dave?

Dave: Yeh.

Mam: What did you have?

Dave: Sausage and chips.

Mam: Any gravy?

Dave: No. Mam couldn't be arsed.

Mam: Well I don't blame her, it's getting near summer.

Dad: All right Dave?

Dave: Yeh.

Dad: How's your dad?

Dave: All right.

Dad: How's his leg?

Dave: It's all right.

Dad: Tell him I was asking for him.

Dave: Have I given you one of my business cards, James?

PASSING DAD CARD.

Dad: What's this, soft lad? (READING CARD) 'You've heard the rest now hear the best . . . Dave Best and Denise Royle . . . Mobile Disco' . . . You've not going to pull many birds with her name on it, are you?

Denise: Shut it, Dad. These are brilliant, Dave.

Dad: How much did these cost?

Dave: Three notes.

Mam: Each.

Dave: No, for fifty . . . Knutsford Service Station . . . I give Tony Macca one, Terry Duckers, Gary . . .

Denise: You're supposed to give them to people you don't know . . . they're all your mates.

Dave: I want them to know I'm doing well, don't I?

Denise: Don't just go wasting them, Dave. Do you want one, Mam?

Mam: Yeh, give me one for me and one for the baker's.

Denise: You're not having one, Antony.

Antony: Hey, and I'm bothered!

ANTONY EXITS.

Denise: Gis another one for me mam.

Dave: I've not got any left.

Dad: I bet Richard Branson is quaking in his books with businessmen like you about.

PAUSE.

Dad: Right, where's the paper . . . I'm going for an Eartha Kitt.

Denise: Ah Dad.

DAD GETS UP AND LEAVES ROOM. PAUSE.

Denise: Cheryl got a gorgeous top off the market today.

Mam: What's it like?

Denise: Blue . . . gorgeous it is.

Mam: Uh, sounds lovely. Are you getting one?

Denise: Yeh.

Mam: Get me one as well then.

Denise: Hey mam, you know my suede boots out of the catalogue . . . I don't want them anymore, buckle's broke. Do you want them?

Mam: Yeh. You haven't finished paying for them yet?

Denise: Doesn't matter.

Mam: Shall I pay the rest?

Denise: Yeh, all right. (TO DAVE) What are you doing? Are we going up Feathers for last hour?

Dave: No. I'm knackered.

Denise: I'm not mithered. We'll just watch telly.

Dave: Is there owt on?

Denise: No.

Dave: Oh, we'll go down Feathers.

Denise: You were knackered a minute a go.

Mam: If he wants to go for a drink, let him go.

Denise: Yeh, but I just asked him and he said he was knackered.

Dave: Do you want to go or what?

Denise: I wanted to go in the first place. I'm not going now anyway . . . you've annoyed me.

UNCOMFORTABLE SILENCE. DAD ENTERS.

Dad: Hey, take my advice . . . no one go in that lavatory for at least half an hour.

Denise: Dad we've got company.

Dad: It's only Dave . . . he's as bad.

Denise: Why can't you just go to the toilet without announcing it? Why do we always have to know about it?

Dad: I'm only making conversation . . . what's up with you?

Denise: We can make do without, thanks all the same.

PAUSE DURING WHICH DAD IS UNCOMFORTABLE ON HIS CHAIR.

Dad: Why do you keep buying that cheap toilet paper . . . it's cutting my arse to ribbons?

Denise: Mam tell him! He's doing it on purpose now.

Mam: When I was buying the dear stuff you complained.

Dad: I didn't.

Mam: You did. You said you might as well wipe your arse with pound notes.

Dad: (REMEMBERING) Oh yeh, I did didn't I.

MAM AND DAD LAUGH. PAUSE.

Denise: So are you coming down the Feathers or what?

Dave: I thought you said we weren't going.

Denise: Yeh, well, he's doing my head in.

Antony: (ENTERING) Who's stunk that toilet out?

Mam: Who do you think?

Dad: That's what it's there for in't it? Where do you want me to have a shit? You'd soon complain it I had a crap in the kitchen.

AT NO TIME DURING THE DIALOGUE BELOW DO WE ACTUALLY SEE OUT OF THE WINDOW.

Antony: (AT WINDOW) Hey look, Jacko's got a new motor.

Dave: (COMING TO WINDOW) That's not new, that's L-reg.

Denise: (NOW AT WINDOW) Oh 'ere y'are, here's Lorraine

coming out to look at it. She never has them leggings off her. Mam come and look at Lorraine looking at Jacko's car in her leggings.

Mam: (COMING TO WINDOW) She never wears nowt but them leggings, her.

Dad: (STILL SITTING) That's how come they can afford a new car.

Mam: Oh, look at Carol over the road gawping through the window. You'd think she'd never seen a car before.

Denise: She's not going to drive it in her slippers is she?

Dave: He's not going to let her drive that, she's always bladdered.

Denise: How much more can you look at a car? Look at her getting the manual out . . . as if she knows what she's looking at.

Dad: (FROM CHAIR) What sort of car is it, Antony?

Antony: Sierra.

Dad: What, an estate?

Antony: No saloon.

Dad: Is it a hatchback?

Antony: Come and look yourself.

Dad: You're one lazy little sod you.

Mam: It's a red one, Jim.

Dad: What's the bodywork like?

Mam: I've just told you it's red.

Dad: Thank you, Jeremy Clarkson.

DAD REMAINS SEATED WATCHING TELLY.

Dave: I'm going to go and wind them up . . . tell him he's been ripped off big style.

Denise: You don't know how much he's paid for it.

Dave: (EXITING) I'm just going to wind him up aren't I . . . whatever he says it's too much right.

Antony: (FOLLOWING DAVE) Hey I'm watching this.

PAUSE.

Dave: Hey, Jacko . . .

Mam: Oh look at them windows . . . when did he last come, Jim?

Denise: Look at Dave, he's got absolutely no arse.

Mam: In't our Antony gangly. I'm not gangly and Jim's not gangly. I don't know where that's come from.

Denise: I'm not gangly.

Mam: You're never gangly.

Denise: I'm going to have a bath. Mam, go and check if the toilet still smells from him.

Mam: Oh, you can chance it now, love.

Denise: I'm not breathing in.

DENISE EXITS. MAM SITS DOWN.

Dad: Y'know my Dad'd been dead twenty years tomorrow? He was only the same age as me when he died.

Mam: Shut up, Jim. Stop being so maudlin.

Dad: Mind you, he was a shithouse with me mother.

Mam: You shouldn't speak ill of the dead.

Dad: Your mother won't have long now I bet.

Mam: Jim!

Dad: Well, she's had a good innings.

Mam: You're a miserable sod at times you. What sort of thing is that to say?

Dad: Uh, I think I've cheered myself up. Is there any Penguins left?

Mam: No. Is there owt on, Jim?

Dad: No.

Mam: Shall we have an early night?

Dad: (CHANGING CHANNEL) I'm sure there must be something on.

END OF EPISODE.

Episode 3

Scene 1

<u>INT. AFTERNOON–LIVING ROOM</u>
(DAD, MAM, DENISE, ANTONY, NANA, MARY)

EVERYONE IS SITTING DOWN AFTER THEIR SUNDAY LUNCH, EXCEPT MAM WHO IS CLEARING TABLE.

Nana: That was a lovely dinner, Barbara. You see that's the thing when you live on your own, it's not worth doing a chicken just for one, there's too much for one meal. You see you get four or five meals out of chicken, you're sick of it by Thursday.

Dad: You can just get a chicken breast can't you?

Nana: Well, I'm not that keen on chicken.

Mam: Do you want a cup of tea, Mam, or do you want your stout?

Nana: Uh no, I never have my stout till nine o'clock. A cuppa tea'll do me. I don't drink at all me . . . just a bottle of stout of a night and a sherry at Christmas.

Antony: What about a whisky at New Year, Nana?

Nana: Yes, a whisky at New Year, a sherry at Christmas and a bottle of stout.

Dad: (WINDING HER UP) You'll have champagne at the wedding.

Nana: (FALLLING FOR IT) Yes, champagne at weddings, whisky at New Year, sherry at Christmas and a bottle of stout . . . that'll do me.

MAM LEAVES ROOM.

Nana: Hey Denise, you mam's looking tired.

Denise: No, she's fine.

Nana: Do you think she's taking too much on, what with the baker's and all you lot?

Denise: No, she's sound.

Mam: (RETURNING WITH CAKES) I've got us a little treat.

Nana: (TAKING CAKE) Ooh, I love cream cakes me.

Mam: They're a little damaged but they taste the same.

Dad: They taste better 'cos they're free. (PAUSE WHILST DAD TAKES A MOUTHFUL) Could you damage us an egg custard next week, will you Barb?

Denise: Mam, don't give me one of them cakes. I've Mary coming round from next door with my wedding dress.

Dad: You won't put weight on that fast.

Denise: Yeh, give us one of them eclairs.

Antony: (ENTERING) Is there cakes on the go?

Mam: Antony, take the bin out, that chicken'll start to smell if you leave it.

Antony: (EATING) Ahh Mam, I haven't sat down. What about lazy arse there?

Mam: There's too much swearing in this house, that's you Jim, you taught them that.

Dad: Mi'arse.

MARY POPS HER HEAD ROUND THE DOOR.

Mary: Hello, it's only me.

Everyone: Hello Mary.

Mary: Oh hello Norma, how are you keeping?

Nana: Not too bad considering.

Mam: Have you had a Sunday dinner, Mary?

Mary: No, I've not bothered. That's the mood I'm in. (BOTH MAM AND MARY LAUGH) Dave's not here then? I'll go and get Cheryl and we'll bring the dress.

Mam: Oh sit yourself down Mary, we'll phone her.

Dad: It's only next door. Antony you go. (TO NANA) Ninety-eight quid that last bill cost.

Nana: They're not cheap are they, phones . . . specially when you live on your own. I was going to get that Friends and Family but I couldn't make up the numbers . . . most of them are dead.

Dad: (GETTING UP) I'll do the pots.

Nana: I'll tell you who has died . . .

CUT TO:

Scene 2

<u>INT. SUNDAY AFTERNOON–KITCHEN</u>
(DAD, ANTONY, CHERYL, DAVE)

DAD PUTTING POTS INTO SINK. ANTONY ENTERS.

Dad: Do you want to wash or do the drying?

Antony: Neither.

Dad: Right, you're drying.

Antony: I'd sooner wash.

Dad: I'm sorry, I'm going to have to take your first answer.

PAUSE.

Antony: (STARTING TO DRY) Nana don't half give it some of that. (GESTURING WITH HIS HAND THAT SHE TALKS TOO MUCH)

Dad: Hey lad, have some respect, that's your grandmother . . . mind you, you're right.

CHERYL KNOCKS AND ENTERS.

Cheryl: Hiya.

Dad: Hiya luv.

Cheryl: Are they in there?

Dad: Yeh, they've got the cauldron out.

CHERYL EXITS THROUGH OTHER DOOR.

Antony: What was Grandad like?

Dad: Your mum's dad? (AFTER SOME THOUGHT) Hard of hearing, the lucky bleeder.

Antony: What did he do?

Dad: He was the finest free-hand tool-grinder I've ever seen in my life.

Antony: What's a tool-grinder?

Dad: Don't worry your head son, they won't have one in McDonald's time you start.

Antony: (TO DAD) You haven't done the roasting pan.

Dad: You have to leave that till . . . your mother's got a chance to do it.

Antony: What was he like though, Grandad?

Dad: Sound fellow, liked his ale, always paid his way, stood his corner, paid half towards our wedding not like Ebenezer.

Antony: Who's Ebenezer?

Dad: Dave's dad . . . Hopalong Cassidy.

DAVE ENTERS FROM HALL DOOR TO DAD'S SURPRISE.

Dave: All right Jim, Ant.

Dad: All right cock.

Dave: I've been sent in here. She's trying the dress on. She won't let me look at it.

Dad: I'll let you have a look at the bill if you want to.

Dave: I feel rough today me, my guts are off. I had a bad pint last night.

Dad: I bet you washed it down with a few more didn't you?

Antony: How do you know it's a bad pint?

Dave: Cos you end up shitting through the eye of a needle.

Dad: Where did you go?

Dave: The Pear Tree.

Dad: You don't want to drink there.

Dave: I know that now don't I!

Dad: He don't clean his pumps, him.

Antony: The lager's all right.

Dad: How would you know that, soft lad?

Antony: Dad, I'm fifteen!

Dad: All right, but if I catch you in the Feathers I'll clip your earhole. You don't shit on your own doorstep.

Dave: I nearly did last night. I couldn't get the key in quick enough.

Dad: So what are you doing tonight?

Dave: Back down the Pear Tree, I'm doing the quiz night.

Dad: How much they paying you?

Dave: Twenty notes and all you can drink.

Dad: Just twenty notes then.

Antony: Why don't you tell me the answers?

Dave: You only win a T-shirt.

Antony: Better on my back.

Dave: Anyway they'll know it's a fix if you win, you don't know nowt.

Antony: I know not to drink the bitter in there.

DAD AND ANTONY LAUGH.

CUT TO:

Scene 3

INT. SUNDAY AFTERNOON–LIVING ROOM
(MAM, DENISE, NANA, CHERYL, DAD, MARY)

DENISE STANDS ON COFFEE-TABLE IN WEDDING DRESS SMOKING A CIGARETTE. MAY IS PINNING THE HEM.

Mam: Ahh, you look absolutely gorgeous.

Denise: Hey, do you remember Genette's wedding with that ironing mark down the back of her dress? Everyone was laughing. She didn't give a toss. She said it wouldn't show up on the photos.

Cheryl: Hey Denise, make sure I catch the bouquet. I'm going to stand well to your right . . . which'll be your left when you turn round.

Mam: How's your diet going, Cheryl?

Cheryl: I'm doing all right. I lost four pounds, I put two back on, then another two . . . so I've not gained any.

Mam: You're doing very well to stick to it.

Nana: Where is it you're going again?

Denise: Tenerife.

Nana: That'll be gorgeous. Me and your grandad went for a week in Blackpool in a B&B. It's a Harry Ramsden's now . . . quite fitting as we met in a fish shop. It was after the Town Hall dance, I was with my friend Betty, she married a joiner . . . moved to Leeds. He used to knock her about a bit . . . but her home was lovely.

Mary: Do you ever hear from her, Norma?

Nana: No, I never liked her . . . even when we were best friends. (PAUSE) What are you wearing, Cheryl?

Mary: It's a lovely dusky peach dress. We've just got to let it out a couple of inches.

DAD POPS HIS HEAD ROUND THE DOOR THEN ENTERS.

Dad: How long's this lot going on in here? You're got five minutes to *Antiques Roadshow*.

Mam: Jim!

MEANING 'LOOK AT DRESS'.

Dad: Sorry, luv . . . look at you. That dress is absolutely gorgeous. Don't scratch that coffee-table. Hey, do you remember Genette with that ironing mark on her back?

Mam: We were just talking about that.

Dad: Remember her bridesmaid tried to stand right up behind her throughout the ceremony.

Denise: What's Dave doing?

Dad: Talking us through the shits he had last night.

Mam: (FEARING HE'LL SEE THE DRESS) Don't let him in here.

Dad: It's all right he's firmed up now. (PAUSE) You've got five minutes . . . when that *Antiques Roadshow* music starts we're in here, dress or no dress.

DAD EXITS.

Denise: Are you done now, Mary?

Mary: Yes, I'll finish the hem tonight.

Denise: Cheryl, come up and help me get this off me.

DENISE AND CHERYL EXIT.

Mam: Ah, you feel for them don't you, Mary . . . their whole married lives before them.

Mary: (SIGH) Yeh, you know nothing of pain.

Nana: I hope they make it all right, it's not easy is it? I was unhappy for twenty-five years but at least I gave it a try.

CUT TO:

Scene 4

INT. AFTERNOON–KITCHEN
(DAVE, DAD, JOE, MARY, ANTONY)

DAD ENTERS.

Dave: What's the dress like?

Dad: I don't know. It's a wedding dress in't it. Tell you what, she looks bloody gorgeous. Bloody hell, here comes Mastermind. (DAD OPENS THE DOOR) All right Joe, you busy?

Joe: No.

Dad: Are you looking for Mary?

Joe: No.

Dad: Right . . . Are you having a brew?

Joe: No, I won't thanks.

Dad: Do you want a damaged cake?

Joe: (AFTER A BIT OF AFTERTHOUGHT) Aye, go on then.

Dad: Do you go up the Pear Tree, Joe?

Joe: No. (PAUSE) I don't like the bitter.

Dave: Neither does my bumhole, it's like a chewed orange.

Dad: (STRUGGLING FOR CONVERSATION) *Antiques Roadshow*'s on in a minute.

Joe: Oh aye?

Dad: Barbara's mother's down, why don't you nip through and say hello.

Joe: No.

PAUSE.

Dad: So life treating you all right, is it?

Joe: Can't complain. (PAUSE) Nice bit of cake.

Dave: Did you hear the thunder last night?

Joe: No.

Dave: Slept right through it then?

Joe: Must have done.

Dad: Antony, nip through and see if we can go in.

MARY ENTERS.

Mary: You're all right to go in now. Oh Dave, you're in for a treat. (TO JOE) Are you stopping, Joe?

Joe: No.

MARY AND JOE EXIT.

Dad: Bloody hell, he's hard work ain't he?

Dave: I wonder if he'd give me any tips for my wedding speech.

CUT TO:

Scene 5

INT. EVENING–LIVING ROOM
(DAD, MAM, NANA, DENISE, DAVE, ANTONY, VOICE ON TV)

MAM, ANTONY AND DAVE ENTER AND SIT DOWN.

Nana: Do you think she's all right, Barbara? She's not getting too down about this wedding?

Mam: No, she's bearing up very well, Mam.

Dave: Are you all right, Nana?

ANTIQUES ROADSHOW MUSIC IS HEARD ON THE TV. DURING THIS SCENE THE TV IS HEARD BENEATH THE SPEECH BUT WE NEVER SEE THE SCREEN.

Nana: Ohh, I do like what's his name.

Mam: Hugh Scully.

Nana: I'll watch anything with him on.

Dad: He's on then . . . let's hear him. (REACHING INTO HIS POCKET) All right get your twenty p's out if you're having a bet.

DENISE ENTERS.

Denise: (TO DAVE) Hiya Dave.

Dave: Shh, I'm watching this.

Mam: (PASSING DAD 20P) Cheryl took the dress has she?

Dad: Who's in?

Dave: Here y'are.

Dad: (INSPECTING TOP OF TV) We're still light. Antony?

Antony: Mam, lend us a quid.

Mam: No you're too young for gambling.

Nana: I'll give it you . . . split the winnings though.

Dad: Denise?

Denise: I'm sharing Dave's.

Dad: You can only have one guess.

Dave: All right, I'll put in for her an'all.

Dad: That's true love . . . penny bun cost you tuppence.

Denise: Ugh, I'm crap on pottery.

Mam: It's got a crack on it that should make it cheaper.

Nana: We had a cupboard full of them.

Dad: How much did you pay for them?

Dave: I'm saying hundred and fifty notes. How about you, Denise?

Denise: I'd say that.

Dave: No, you lemon, I've put in for you separate. You've got to say another one.

Antony: Three hundred notes.

Mam: No, never three hundred . . . two eighty.

Nana: Twenty-five quid.

Dad: It's worth more than that, she wouldn't have bothered her arse taking them.

Nana: That's how much I paid for them . . . just after the war it was.

Dad: I'm saying eight-fifty . . . shhh.

Voice on TV: . . . which despite the chip should still fetch one thousand, two hundred pounds.

Dad: (REACTING) Yes! come to Daddy.

HE SCOOPS THE MONEY OFF THE TELLY.

Denise: You were miles out.

Dad: Nearest wins.

Nana: Look at the face on her. She wanted more for it, didn't she Barbara?

Mam: Miserable old so and so.

Dad: Quiet now, we're talking Queen Anne furniture.

Nana: I like that blouse.

Dad: It's the furniture we're interested in.

Nana: We had one of those in the shed.

Mam: You never did?

Nana: Yes . . . bin men took it.

Dad: Come on quick he's winding up. I'm saying two thousand, four hundred pounds.

Dave: You've blobbed it this time Jim, it's double that . . . five thousand.

Antony: Four thousand, nine hundred and ninety-nine.

Dave: Hey, you can't do that?

Antony: I can, can't I, Mam . . . tell him.

Denise: I'm saying three thousand pounds.

Dad: Barbara?

Mam: Oh, I don't know, five thousand.

Dave: I've said that.

Mam: Six thousand then.

Dad: For a manky old table?

Mam: Five hundred then, I'm not bothered.

Dad: Norma?

Nana: They had one on last week made out of lollysticks.

Dad: How much are you saying?

Voice on TV: In the region of two thousand five hundred pounds.

Dad: (REACTING) Yes!

Nana: Two thousand, five hundred pounds.

Dad: Too late now.

Nana: I was going to say that.

Dad: Mi'arse.

Mam: You're a robbing sod.

Dave: I bet he's taped this . . . it'll be a repeat.

PAUSE. PEOPLE PUT 20P'S ON TV DURING SPEECHES BELOW.

Mam: Candelabra . . . here we are.

Nana: We had one of them.

Dad: Mi'arse . . . who do you think you are, the Queen of Sheba?

Dave: I'm saying seven hundred and fifty notes.

Antony: Seven hundred and forty-nine.

Dave: I'm warning you, Nobby.

Denise: Do you think I should put a candelabra on the wedding list . . . not one of these crappy old ones, a new one . . . what do you think Dave?

Dave: What?

Dad: Are we all in or what?

Nana: Ooooh, do you remember the power cuts in the seventies? That would have come in handy.

Dad: Shut up and guess will you.

Mam: Jim, don't be rude.

Dad: I'm not being, there's money here on the go.

Nana: (DURING THIS SPEECH THE VOICE ON THE TV SAYS THE PRICE OF THE CANDELABRA) We used to have candles on saucers all round the house. Ooh, we had to tie the dog up, do you remember Barbara?

Dad: (DISTRAUGHT) We've missed it now! How much did he say?

Mam: I never said how much it was.

Dave: I think he said seven hundred and fifty notes.

Dad: No way.

Denise: How much did he say then?

Dad: We'll never know now will we, with you lot yapping.

Denise: It doesn't make any difference does it . . . we can do a rollover.

Dad: I was on for a hat trick here . . . sod it, I'm going for a Tom Tit.

Nana: Get off.

DAD EXITS.

Mam: He's a big mardy-arse.

Nana: Always has been.

Antony: I'm taking my twenty p back.

Denise: Yeh . . . it's not even yours . . . Nana gave it you.

Antony: I'm going t'shop.

Denise: Get me twenty ciggies.

Antony: Can I keep the change?

Mam: Shout up to your dad to see if he wants some ciggies.

ANTONY GOES TO BOTTOM OF THE STAIRS.

Antony: Dad, do you want some ciggies?

Dad (OOV): (SHOUTING FROM THE TOILET) Yeh, get the money off your mam.

ANTONY RE-ENTERS.

Mam: Tell him to get it out of his winnings.

ANTONY GOES TO THE BOTTOM OF THE STAIRS AGAIN.

Antony (OOV): (SHOUTING) Mam says get it out your winnings.

Dad (OOV): (SHOUTING FROM TOILET) I can't have a shite in peace here.

Mam: Here y'are, Antony.

ANTONY RE-ENTERS AND GETS MONEY OFF HIS MAM.

And get me and Nana a Crunchie. Do you want one, Denise?

Denise: No, I'm cutting back . . . have half with me Dave.

Dave: Yeh.

Mam: (TO ANTONY) Get yourself one and get your dad a Turkish Delight.

ANTONY EXITS.

Nana: Looking forward to the wedding, Dave?

Dave: Oh aye, big style. I can't wait. I'll be hammered by eight o'clock.

Mam: You better not be . . . that's what your stag night's for.

Denise: He's only trying to wind me up, Mam.

Dave: I can have a drink.

Denise: You're not getting hammered, no ways.

Nana: I'll have a glass of sherry and my stout, that'll do me.

Mam: Don't forget your champagne, Mam.

Nana: Oh yeh, a glass of champagne, a glass of sherry and my stout.

DAD RE-ENTERS.

Dave: That was quick.

Dad: You can't have a decent shit in this house, I'll bake it 'til she's gone. (TO NANA) Are you right, Norma? I'll take you on the bus.

Mam: Ah leave her Jim, she's only just settled.

Nana: It's be less trouble if I were dead . . . won't be long now.

Dad: If I'm taking you I've got to go now cos we've got to get to your house on the bus then I've got to get back on the bus so as I can get to the Feathers.

Nana: I don't mind so long as I'm back in time for *Heartbeat* . . . oh I'm not missing that . . . I might as well be dead.

Dad: You've been raising our hopes with that one for the last fifteen years . . . you'll outlive the lot of us.

Mam: She'll outlive you if you don't sit down.

'Ninety-eight quid . . . it's good to talk my arse'

'Cheryl's just been lookin at men's nobs'

Denise

Dave

Mam and Dad

ntony

Nana

Mary and Joe

'Right, any requests?'

'Now, are you two getting married or not?'

'Dave, I love you, y'big pillock'

Watching the telly

'How you fixed for denim . . . feel the quality of that'

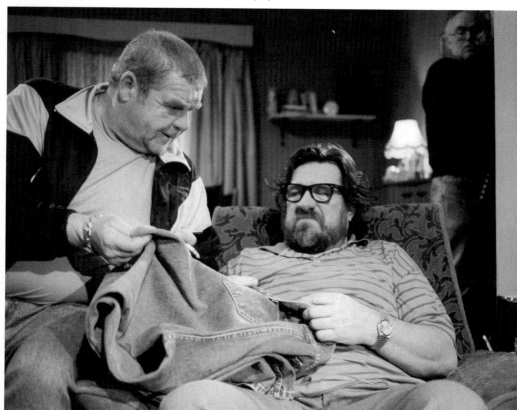

eave it . . . that's the fashionable way to wear these'

You look like a little princess. I'm dead proud of you'

'Dad, giz a ciggi . . . calm my nerves'

Dave: I'll take you in the van, Nana. You'll have to get in the back though.

Nana: Long time since I was in the back of a van. (LAUGHS) You're a good un cock. I'll leave you something nice in my will.

Dave: Why wait 'til then? There's plenty of room in the back of'van when you get out. I've had my eyes on that clock of yours.

Nana: You cheeky begger. Hugh Scully'd give us a few bob for that.

Denise: Can we stop talking about Nana dying?

Dad: Yeh . . . have a little bit of respect, wait until she's gone out the door. I'm only joking, Norma . . . the day you go will be a sad day in this house, (BEAT) if we don't get that clock.

Mam: He hasn't got a heart, he's got a swinging brick.

Nana: I'll tell you who's in hospital. Gwen's husband.

Mam: What's he having done?

Nana: He's having something fitted.

Dad: What, a wardrobe?

Nana: No . . . I don't know . . . but she doesn't think he'll come out again . . . she lost her brother in October. He went to bed after *Inspector Morse* and never woke up again.

Mam: I never liked *Inspector Morse*.

ANTONY COMES BACK AND HANDS OUT CIGGIES AND CHOCOLATE.

Dad: Thanks, gay boy.

Denise: (HANDING DAVE CRUNCHIE) Dave, don't let me have any of that, right.

Antony: Hey Dave, Beverly Macca was in the offie.

Dave: What are you telling me for?

Antony: Well, you fancy her don't you?

Dave: Stop shit-stirring.

Denise: Why does he have to cause trouble?

Antony: She had one of her kids with her . . . looks a lot like you now, Dave.

Mam: Stop it Antony, that's enough.

PAUSE.

Nana: Who's Beverly Macca?

Mam: A girl Dave went out with.

Dave: Only once.

Dad: That's all it takes.

Dave: I did nowt.

Denise: Better not have . . . she's a dirty cow.

Nana: Have I ever seen Beverly Macca?

Mam: No more about Beverly Macca now, we're having a brew.

Dad: Antony, go and make a brew.

Antony: I've just been to the shop.

Dad: The kettle's already boiled lazy arse. Serve you right for stirring.

ANTONY LEAVES ROOM. DENISE GIVES ANTONY A LOOK.

Antony (OOV): Mam.

Mam: Leave him Denise. It's like this all the time in this house.

Nana: At least it's better than being on your own.

Dad: Do you live on your own Norma? . . . You should have said.

Mam: Oh, you're a sarcastic bugger, Jim.

PAUSE.

Dave: (UNWRAPPING CRUNCHIE) Are you sure you didn't want any of this, Denise?

Denise: Eat it quick before I change my mind.

Dave: (EATING SLOWLY) Hmm, lovely chocolate . . . hmmm, honeycomb centre.

Denise: Ah, don't be tight, Dave.

Dave: (OVERACTING) Hmmm, it's the best chocolate bar I've had . . . ever.

Nana: 'Tis nice, in't it.

Denise: Nana! (TO DAVE) Just give us the end of it then.

Dave: No . . . I'm thinking of you.

Denise: No, come on now, I'm not messing.

Dave: No, I'm not taking Bella Emberg down the aisle. (RELENTING) Here y'are.

Denise: No . . . I don't want it now.

DAVE HOLDS IT UP TO HIS MOUTH IN SLOW MOTION, TEASING AS IF HE'S GOING TO EAT IT.

There's something wrong with you.

DAVE EATS LAST BIT.

You ate it! Cheers . . . I'm not marrying you now.

Dave: And I'm bothered!

Mam: That's not a reason not to marry him.

Denise: I'm only joking.

Nana: He'll be back to that Beverly if you're not careful.

ANTONY ENTERS WITH TEAS.

Dave: I only went with her once.

Antony: I'm not saying anything.

Mam: What's that you're giving Nana?

Antony: Tea.

Mam: You know she likes it in a china cup.

Nana: It's all right, I'll make do.

Mam: It's no trouble, Mam, he can change it. Go on, Antony.

ANTONY TUTS HEAVILY AND TAKES MUG AWAY INTO OTHER ROOM.

Dave: I don't want to rush you, Nana, but I'm going to have to get going in a minute. I'm doing a pub quiz at the Pear Tree.

Mam: She hasn't even got her tea yet.

Nana: I can't say I've not had a lovely day . . . that dinner was gorgeous and them broken cakes were lovely.

Mam: I'll give you some of them to take with you.

Nana: I've got Gwen coming round tomorrow on the way back from the hospital . . . that'll be a nice treat for her . . . what with what's going on with her husband . . . take her mind off it for a bit. I can go home and make one for myself.

DAD AND DAVE EXCHANGE A LOOK. ANTONY GIVES NANA HER TEA WHICH IS NOW IN A CHINA CUP. EVERYONE ELSE HAS MUGS.

Mam: (AS SHE LEAVES ROOM) Let me put them in a box for you before I forget.

Nana: Have you go that free paper? You see, Dave, I don't get them delivered where I live.

Dad: That's cos it's local . . . you live the other side of town . . . you get your local one.

Nana: I prefer yours.

Dad: Antony, go and get your nana's coat.

MAM RE-ENTERS.

Mam: (REMEMBERING) Ohh, Mam, that bald comedian you like is back on at the Labour Club.

Nana: Oh he was funny him, weren't he?

Mam: Do you want me to get you a ticket?

Nana: No.

ANTONY STANDS READY WITH NANA'S COAT. DAVE TAKES IT.

Dave: Sorry to rush you, Nana.

Nana: Where's my bag? (SHE KNOCKS BACK HER TEA. TO DAVE) Can you get the cakes, luv?

Denise: What about your paper, Nana?

Nana: Oh yeah and don't forget my stout.

Mam: Antony.

Dad: Bloody hell, are you leaving us anything?

Denise: (TO DAVE) I'll have my face on by the time you get back.

Nana: See you, Jim . . . don't get up.

Dad: (NOT MOVING) Missing you already, Norma.

ANTONY RETURNS WITH STOUT. THERE'S THE USUAL KISSES AND GOODBYES.

Mam: Give us a ring when you get home.

Dad: Dave's taking her home, what can happen to her?

Mam: Take her all the way in, Dave . . . it's like Beirut round there.

Denise: They'll nick the fillings out your mouth round there.

Nana: Jim . . . will you tape me Montel Williams?

Dad: Yes luv. Yes.

ALL BUT DAD AND ANTONY GO TO DOOR.

She always takes half hour to go her. She'll be on the phone for half hour telling us she's got home.

Antony: Has she got a load of antiques?

Dad: Has she my arse!

END OF EPISODE.

Episode 4

Scene 1

<u>INT. DAY–LIVING ROOM</u>
(DAD, MAM, DENISE, ANTONY, DAVE, CHERYL)

DAD'S BIRTHDAY. THERE ARE FIVE BIRTHDAY CARDS UP.
DENISE IS LYING ON THE SOFA. DAD SITS WATCHING TV.
MAM ENTERS WITH A GLASS OF WATER AND TWO
TABLETS.

Mam: Here you are, luv. (OFFERING DENISE TABLETS AND
WATER) How do you feel now?

Denise: I'll tell you where it is . . . it's behind that eye and
behind that eye, across there . . . it won't let up.

Mam: I think it's stress-related.

Dad: Funny how you always get stress after you've had seven-
teen halves of lager.

ANTONY ENTERS.

Mam: You've taken on too much with this wedding, Denise.

Dad: She's got a bloody hangover.

Denise: It's not, it's stress.

Antony: Get up, Denise, I want to sit down.

Denise: Sit somewhere else.

Antony: Why don't you get up and go to bed if you're ill?

Denise: It's freezing up there.

Antony: Why's she doing that voice?

Denise: Because I'm not well.

Antony: You want a psychiatrist.

Mam: You never know with headaches what they can turn into.

Dad: Yeh, a bloody drama.

Mam: Well I think it's a combination of the stress and . . . err . . . something else.

Dad: Ey up, it's Dr Quinn, Medicine Woman.

PAUSE.

Turn telly over, Ant.

Denise: I'm watching this.

Dad: I thought you were busy with headache.

Mam: Leave her alone, Jim, she's got a lot on with this wedding.

Denise: Will you shut up about this wedding?

Dad: It's me who should have headache . . . in my pocket. Peg-leg won't have headache I'll tell you that for nowt.

PAUSE.

Mam: Ahh, show us that card you got off my mam.

Dad: It's on the mantelpiece.

Mam: Pass it to us, Jim.

Dad: (PASSING CARD [WITH A GOLFER ON FRONT] TO MAM) Twenty-five years she's known me. How many times has she seen me play golf?

Mam: It's the sentiment in't it? (READS) Happy Birthday Jim . . . love Norma.

Dad: She's hardly gone overboard on the sentiment. Barbara Cartland's job's safe.

Mam: Was there a fiver in it?

Dad: Yeh . . . same one as I'll be giving her back next month on her birthday. It's a bloody swizz this birthday lark.

Denise: Ah Dad, did you like them socks?

Dad: Yeh.

Denise: I didn't know whether to get you them or a BMW.

Dad: You did right, luv.

DOORBELL GOES.

Denise: That'll be Dave . . . get it, Ant.

Antony: Kiss my arse.

Dad: Ey.

Denise: (AFFECTING SICKBED VOICE) Ah, will you let him in, Dad?

Dad: Kiss my arse.

Mam: Antony, get the door.

Antony: (GOING TO THE DOOR) I'm sick of her. As soon as she goes the better.

Mam: Take no notice. You're always welcome back here if it doesn't work out.

DAVE ENTERS.

Mam: Hiya Dave.

Dave: Hiya Barbara.

Mam: Have you had your tea, Dave?

Dave: Yeh.

Mam: What did you have?

Dave: Liver and onions.

Mam: Uh, I can't be doing with liver.

Dave: What's up with your face-ache?

Denise: (DOING SICKBED VOICE) I've got a really bad migraine.

Antony: She's doing that voice again.

Dave: I'm not surprised you're bad, you were paralytic last night.

Dad: I told you.

Dave: You had a right gob on you an'all. You're not supposed to give the landlord grief when you get a lock-in.

Mam: Oh Denise, you had me running round . . . like a blue-arse fly . . . you were the same last week.

Dave: Hey Ant, what happened? (MEANING THE BLACK EYE).

Denise: He was in a fight.

Dave: He came second then, didn't he . . . who was it?

Denise: He won't tell.

Dave: Probably a girl.

Antony: It was a gang actually.

Dave: What, the Spice Girls?

Mam: I don't know why people have to fight.

Denise: It's always men.

Dave: What about that time you smacked Beverly Macca.

Denise: She was asking for it.

Mam: Anyway, no more talk of fighting. I'm bringing Dad's cake in. (GOING OUT THE DOOR TO THE KITCHEN) Dim the lights, turn the telly off.

Dad: There's no need for that.

Mam: Denise, come in here and help me.

Dad: How big is this cake?

DENISE EXITS.

Dad: I can't do with all this palaver, me.

MAM ENTERS WITH A VICTORIA SPONGE WITH ONE CANDLE. DENISE FOLLOWS HER IN WITH PLATES. EVERYONE SINGS HAPPY BIRTHDAY.

Denise: Blow it out, Dad.

Dad: Will I buggery, there's another five minutes on that . . . save the lecki.

DAD BLOWS THE CANDLE OUT. THEY ALL CHEER HALF-HEARTEDLY.

Dad: Put the light back on now, Antony, that's enough celebration for one year.

MAM CUTTING IT UP.

Antony: I love birthday cake.

Denise: It's only Victoria Sponge.

Mam: Well, you have to pay for proper birthday cake.

Dad: Hey Barbara, don't take all the mystique out of my birthday cake.

Mam: Denise, nip out and get that Pomagne from the fridge.

DENISE GOES TO THE DOOR.

Dad: Bring us me ciggies when you're up.

Denise: Hey, shove a brush up my arse and I'll sweep the floor.

DENISE EXITS.

Mam: Do you want some cake, Dave?

Dave: No, you're all right.

Mam: Go on, have some . . . it's Jim's birthday.

Dave: All right then.

DENISE RE-ENTERS WITH POMAGNE.

Mam: I'm cutting you a small bit, Denise.

Denise: Right, ta Mam.

Mam: We need the glasses. (UNDOES THE CHINA CABINET) These are dusty, aren't they? (SHE BLOWS THEM AND GIVES THEM A WIPE ON THE SIDE OF HER SKIRT) The Pomagne'll wash that off.

Dad: Here we go, the jolly old birthdays.

DAD OPENS THE POMAGNE WITH A POP.

All: Hurray!

DAD POURS. MARY ENTERS.

Mam: Oh Mary, you must have heard the pop of the champagne.

MAM AND MARY LAUGH.

Dad: (DRY) This is turning out to be the best birthday ever.

Mary: Happy Birthday Jim. (KISSES DAD).

Dad: Cheers, Mary – giftwrapped as well.

Mam: Here, Mary. (OFFERING MUG OF POMAGNE) You'll have to have a mug. In't it awful, we've not got enough glasses.

Mary: Uh, it's only me. (LAUGHS)

Dad: You'd sup it out of a sweaty sock, wouldn't you, Mary.

Mary: You know me too well don't you, Jim? (LAUGHS).

Mam: Here y'are luv, you don't need a plate.

MAM GIVES MARY CAKE. MARY STANDS WITH CAKE IN ONE HAND, CUP IN OTHER.

Dave: Speech.

Dad: (MOCK GRANDEUR) Well, I'd just like to thank everyone for coming . . . for this auspicious occasion. I'd especially like to thank my good wife Barbara for all the hard work she's put in getting that cake from the bakery.

All: (APART FROM MAM) Hurray!

Dad: I'd like to thank Denise . . . for forgetting her hangover.

Dave and Antony: Hurray!

Denise: (DEFENSIVE) The tablets have worked. It was a migraine.

Mary: Have you got a migraine?

Dad: I'd also like to thank my son Antony . . . in advance . . . for getting off his big fat arse and washing the pots.

All: (APART FROM ANTONY) Hurray!

JOE ENTERS.

Dad: And here's the icing on the cake.

Mary: Joe, it's Jim's birthday.

Joe: Aye.

Mary: Well?

Joe: Happy Birthday Jim.

Dad: Cheers Joe . . . you've missed a fabulous speech.

Joe: Have I?

Mam: We've got no cake left. I'll get you a Kit-kat.

MAM GOES FOR BISCUIT BARREL.

Dad: (TO MAM) Get Joe a lager . . . Mary supped all the Pomagne . . . (TO JOE) It's only that nat's piss Barbara got in bulk.

Mary: Where's our Cheryl? She's missing all the fun.

MAM GIVES JOE A KIT-KAT. SHE GOES INTO THE KITCHEN FOR LAGER.

Dad: Your birthday soon in't it, Joe?

Joe: Yeh.

Dad: Doing anything special?

Joe: No.

Dad: Ah well, something to look forward to, isn't it.

MAM RETURNS WITH CAN OF CHEAP LAGER.

Mary: Antony, look at me. Have you got a black eye?

Mam: He's been fighting again, Mary.

Mary: Where did you get that?

Antony: In the precinct.

Denise: Hey Mary, has Cheryl had that jacket from the catalogue yet?

Mary: Yes, she's got it this morning. Cheryl's doesn't fit her. She's dead upset . . . don't say anything. She thinks the size's wrong. She says it's American sizes.

Mam: How's her diet going?

Mary: Oh, she was doing great all day yesterday and then she had a fish supper.

Mam: How's your Kit-kat, Joe?

Joe: Nice.

Mam: How about the lager?

Joe: Nice.

Mary: Will you be celebrating in the Feathers tonight?

Dad: Oh aye . . . it's non-stop. Are you going for a jar, Joe?

Joe: What time will you be in?

Dad: All night.

Joe: No.

Mam: Let's have a photo. Let me get me camera. (MAM GETS CAMERA OUT OF DRAWER) Bunch up everybody. Mary get in there. What are you doing?

Denise: I'm putting some lippy on.

Mam: You don't need lippy on. Antony, stand sideways – I don't want to get that bruise in. All right, smile.

SHE TAKES A PHOTO BUT THERE'S NO FLASH. EVERYONE STAYS IN PLACE WHILST MAM MESSES WITH CAMERA.

Denise: It's not flashing.

Mam: In't it?

Dave: Is the flash switched on? . . . You've got to wait for it to warm up.

Dad: Is there any film in, Barbara?

Mam: Shut up Jim. (POINTING CAMERA) Smile.

EVERYONE SMILES WEAK SMILES.

Mam: You know I've got a feeling they're not going to come out . . . they didn't come out last time.

Denise: What's in the front of that film, Mam.

Mam: Pauline's baby's christening.

Dad: Bloody hell, he's having his twenty-first soon. What's the sell-by date on that film?

Mam: He's not even one yet, Jim.

Mary: Let me take one of just the family.

MARY AND MAM CHANGE PLACES BUT JOE STILL STANDS IN PICTURE.

Mary: Everyone say cheese.

All: (HALF-HEARTEDLY) Cheese.

Mary: I can't turn it on.

Mam: (RESCUING CAMERA) It's the end of the film, Mary.

Mary: I think I've clicked twice on that last one.

Dad: Is it a twenty-four or a thirty-six?

Mam: I don't know.

Dad: Well what number's it on?

Mam: I don't know – it's rewound.

Mary: It's a nice camera that, Barbara.

Mam: It's from Argos . . . we got that for . . . what did we get that for, Jim?

Dad: For taking bloody photographs.

Mam: Ignore him.

Mary: Well, better get back . . . there's *Ruth Rendell* on . . . Are you all right Joe?

Joe: Yeh.

MARY AND JOE MAKE TO LEAVE.

Denise: Ah Mary, send Cheryl in with me jacket will you . . . I'm dying to see what it's like.

Mary: (EXITING) Right luv.

MARY AND JOE EXIT.

Dad: One good thing about those two . . . they don't spoil another pair. (TO DAVE) How's work then, lad?

Dave: I had a job in Blakely this morning . . . four flights of stairs for some shitty old wardrobe and a chest of drawers.

Dad: That's what you're paid for in't it?

Dave: Yeh, but you want a bit of job satisfaction don't you?

Dad: Did you get a tip?

Dave: She gave us a bathroom cabinet. I had to unscrew it from the wall though.

Denise: We're not having any shitey second-hand stuff . . . I'm having everything new from Ikea.

Dave: In your dreams. I can't afford them sort of prices.

Dad: I bet you get a load of tips don't you?

Dave: I get the odd fiver. It's the rich ones that are the tightest . . . it's the poor dears that haven't got two ha'pennies to rub together that want to drop you a couple of quid.

Dad: And you take it!

Dave: Dead right. I'll give you a tip, Jim. Always have a big top pocket and when your hands are full they can drop it in there. Oh aye, you've got to be on the ball in this game.

CHERYL ENTERS WITH LEATHER JACKET IN HER HAND.

Denise: Ohh . . . my jacket . . . I've been gagging for it.

Cheryl: Happy birthday Jim.

Dad: Ta.

Cheryl: What've you given me mam, she's gone giddy as a kipper?

Mam: She's had a mug of Pomagne.

Cheryl: Uh, I love Pomagne.

Mam: Sorry luv, there's none left . . . there's a can of lager going begging.

Cheryl: No thanks Barbara, I'm dieting.

SILENCE AS THEY ALL LOOK AT EACH OTHER.

My mam's sponsoring me.

Dad: How much do you owe her?

Denise: (WEARING JACKET) Uh, it's gorgeous this.

Cheryl: Mine didn't fit me. It's the sizes, they're all to cock.

Denise: But this is a twelve and it fits me.

Cheryl: Yeh the twelves are all right . . . it's the fourteens . . . I think they must have got a bad batch.

Mam: It's dead smart that Denise. Is it leatherlook?

Denise: Is it 'eck . . . it's real leather . . . have a smell. Uh, I'm made up with it, I really am . . . what do you reckon, Dave?

Dave: How much was it?

Denise: You're just like mi dad . . . nothing, it's out a catalogue.

Dave: You've still got to pay for it an't you?

Cheryl: Forty weeks at five pound fifteen.

Denise: Don't be telling him . . . that's my business.

Dad: (HAVING FINALLY WORKED IT OUT) Two hundred and some'at quid!

Denise: Dad, you're taking all the fun out of it.

Dad: Where do you get that kind of money from?

Dave: Me.

Denise: Get lost . . . when was the last time I had anything new?

Mam: Here Denise, let me try it on. I might have one.

Dad: Have you come into money, luv?

MAM TRIES JACKET ON.

Mam: Uh, what do you think, Jim . . . shall I have one of these?

Dad: You'd look lovely in anything, luv . . . why waste two hundred quid?

Denise: You're as tight as a camel's arse in a sandstorm.

Dad: Who's birthday is it?

Antony: It's all right that jacket.

Denise: What you after, being nice to me?

Antony: Shove it up your arse then.

Mam: Ey! Cut it out it's your dad's birthday . . . we don't want arses everywhere.

Dad: Correct.

PAUSE.

Denise: Hey Dave, give us that. (TAKING A SECTION OF DAVE'S PAPER) Hey Dad, it says here . . . if today's your birthday . . . it says (READING) one of the luckiest years of your life for money and love. Utilize your brain and brawn to go even further than anticipated.

Mam: Ooh Jim, that sounds good.

Denise: What are you, Cheryl?

Cheryl: Pisces.

Denise: Sexy and desirable, that's you throughout today. Whether you realize it or not you radiate an aura which can only be described as delectable.

SILENCE AS EVERYONE TAKES IN THE OBVIOUS INACCURACY OF THE FORECAST.

Dad: Spot on again there.

Denise: Dad.

Dad: Cheryl knows I'm joking . . . I've never seen such an aura of delectableness.

Dave: What's mine?

Denise: (PRETENDING TO READ) This week you are ruled by Uranus. Don't be mean with money. If someone you love gets new leather don't moan about the price.

Mam: Is that Russell Grant? . . . He's very good.

Dad: He's as camp as Christmas.

Denise: What if he is?

Dad: He's someone to talk to about Uranus.

DAVE, DAD AND ANTONY LAUGH.

Denise: I'll tell you who else is gay.

Dave: Who?

Denise: Antony.

Antony: Get real.

Dave: Richard Gere's gay.

Denise: No way.

Dave: I'm telling you, it's common knowledge down the Feathers.

Dad: Oh right . . . you mean that showbiz Mecca . . . they've got a direct line to Hollywood in the bar.

Mam: He's married to Cindy Crawford.

Dave: No he split up over . . .

Denise: Over what?

Dave: Over Easter.

Denise: No, what did they split up over?

Dave: Cos he's a fruit, in't he?

Mam: (MISSING THE POINT) And he's now with Russell Grant is he?

Dad: (DOING UP HIS COLLAR) So . . . Cindy Crawford's free is she?

Denise: You've got more chance with Russell Grant.

Mam: I don't care what anybody is . . . whether they're gay, straight, Australian. It's what they're like as a person that counts.

Dad: Steady on Barbara, it's not Live Aid, it's my birthday.

Mam: Shut up Jim, you're a sarcastic bugger . . . (OPENING PACKET) Anyone want a Polo?

Denise: Yeh, giz one of them, Mam.

Antony: I'll have one, I love Polo's.

Mam: Are you having one, Dave?

Dave: No thanks.

Mam: Jim . . . do you want a birthday Polo?

Dad: Aye go on then . . . give us two, make up for the hole.

Mam: Who's not got a Polo? Cheryl, you've not got one.

Cheryl: No, I'm on a diet.

Mam: There's no calories in a Polo, they're only mint. I suck these all day at work.

Dad: The hours must fly by.

Cheryl: Go on then . . . I'll have one to be sociable.

Mam: Come on Dave, there's only you not sucking.

PAUSE WHILST WE HEAR THE SOUND OF EVERYONE SUCKING THEIR POLOS. ANTONY CRUNCHES HIS.

Denise: I can hear you crunching yours from here.

Mam: Did you see that programme on last night about the Kennedy assassination?

Cheryl: No.

Mam: Ohh, that Jackie Bouvier Kennedy . . . she had some lovely clothes.

Antony: Ey Dad, where were you when Kennedy was shot? Everyone's supposed to know.

Dad: (FEIGNING SHOCK) Kennedy was shot! . . . I don't know but wherever it was there's a good chance our immersion was on.

Denise: I'm having a bath.

Dave: Where were you, Barbara?

Mam: Uh, it was before I'd met Jim. I was in the flicks with Charlie Rogers and they interrupted the picture.

Dave: What was it?

Mam: Well, Kennedy had been shot.

Dave: No what was the picture.

Dad: Difficult to see from the back row.

Mam: You never liked Charlie did you? He had a car.

Dad: It was his dad's.

Mam: You didn't have one.

Dad: Why didn't you marry him then?

Mam: Oh no, he had bushy eyebrows.

Dad: Why the bloody hell didn't God give me bushy eyebrows?

Denise: I wish you had married that Charlie bloke . . . he'd have let us have the immersion on.

Mam: He emigrated to Australia.

Dad: He wouldn't need the immersion out there . . . that's why he went.

Denise: You're a tight arse.

Dad: It costs me five quid every time you take a bath. Take a tip from Antony, he doesn't cost me nowt.

Dave: B.O. Bill.

Denise: What, smelly arse?

Mam: Come on now, it's your dad's birthday . . . there's too many arses in this house.

Denise: Actually, I don't think I'll have time to have a bath now if we're going to the Feathers.

Dad: So what you put the immersion heater on for? Antony, get a bath you smelly arse.

Denise: Dad . . . it's not his birthday (LAUGHS) . . . What time are we going to the Feathers?

Dad: Soon as you're ready.

Cheryl: I'll nip home and make myself beautiful.

Dad: You're just coming for last orders then. (LAUGHS)

CHERYL LEAVES.

Denise: Why are you so tight to Cheryl, Dad?

Dad: What's up with you? . . . I'm only joking.

Denise: Well she's dead conscious about what she looks like. Why do you think she's always on a diet?

Dad: Right, I'm saying nowt me. Antony switch over.

PAUSE.

Dave: Did you see the boxing, Jim?

Dad: (ENTHUSIASTIC) Yeh, he ruddy murdered him.

Dave: He kept getting up though . . . silly arse. He should have stayed down . . . still have got the money. If I was in there with that ugly pig I'd have took a dive.

Antony: So would I, no messing.

Dave: You wouldn't last two minutes . . . the Milky Bar Kid.

Antony: You should have seen me last night with the Beswick brothers.

Denise: The Beswick brothers? . . . One's twelve and the other one's fourteen. (LAUGHS) Was it in the sandpit?

Antony: One's fifteen and the other's fourteen and a half actually.

Denise: One can't be fifteen and one fourteen and half, stupid, that doesn't even add up.

Dave: Is that the gang then? Hardly the Krays are they? Did they hit you with their rattle?

Antony: They're hard them two when they're together.

Dad: You want to get them when they're on their own then and give them a good hiding.

Antony: Well they're never on their own, are they?

Dad: What, they don't shit out of the same arsehole do they?

Mam: Arse again.

MAM TAKES CIGARETTE AND LIGHTS UP. DAD LIGHTS UP AS WELL.

Mam: Uh, I never told you, when I went to get your dad's jumper . . . do you know who's working in Marks's now? . . . Sheila Cowles . . . she's divorced now, she's lost four stone, had her roots done, she's had her ears pierced twice . . . Uh, she looks gorgeous.

CHERYL ENTERS WEARING TOO MUCH MAKE-UP.

Dad: Who is this delectable young lady with an aura? Can it be? It's not Cheryl from next door?

Denise: Dad, leave her.

Mam: Oh I like the way you've done your eyes. What is it?

Cheryl: It's Boots's own, Number Seven.

Dave: (JOKING) And what's on the other eye?

Dad: So are we going or what? It's thirsty work this birthday lark.

Denise: Hang on Dad, I've not got me lippy on.

Dave: Can I kip here tonight, Barbara? I don't want to drive when I'm bladdered.

Mam: No, you're right to.

Dave: Yeh, I got caught last time didn't I . . . banned for a year . . . nightmare.

Denise: Anyway Dave, I'm taking up driving soon. You'll have to get me a little runaround.

Dad: I thought they were trying to keep death off the roads.

Denise: (APPLYING MAKE-UP) Get lost, it can't be that bad. Dave drives.

Antony: I'm going to get a motorbike, me.

Mam: You don't want a motorbike, they're deathtraps.

Denise: (PUTTING ON LIPPY) Yeh let him have one, Mam, don't be tight . . . Dad, lend us a fiver to get you a drink.

Dad: I haven't got it kid, you'll have to ask your mam.

Denise: What about that fiver you got off Nana?

Dad: I've budgeted for that. (PASSING OVER FIVER) Ey up, if you were any sharper you'd cut yourself. (BECOMING DELIB-ERATELY OVER-GENEROUS) Anyway . . . I'll get the first round in for my lovely family, one and all, who want to celebrate my birthday.

Cheryl: Am I in that round?

Dad: What do you drink?

Cheryl: Bacardi and Diet Coke.

Dad: You're not strictly family, are you luv . . . course you are . . . aura and all.

Antony: Can I come?

Mam: I don't think so, luv.

Dad: Let him come . . . he can sit in the corner. Ted won't mind . . . if there's any trouble Ant can wade in, big style.

Antony: I'm not having shandy . . . I'm having lager.

Dad: Fascinating as this is . . . I think you've forgotten the birthday boy and the copious amounts of ale that he's going to put away in his big belly without a doubt . . . put your coat on, Barbara.

Mam: Why, are you taking me with you?

Dad: No, I'm turning the fire off . . . of course I'm taking you with me . . . as if I'd leave you here on my birthday . . . come on . . . don't forget your purse.

END OF EPISODE.

Episode 5

Scene 1

<u>INT. NIGHT–BEDROOM</u>
(MAM, DAD, DAVE, DENISE, ANTONY)

MAM IS SITTING AT DRESSING TABLE SLAPPING NIVEA ON. DAD IS IN BED.

Mam: I'm holding that place together. I did four trays of pasties before Tittyfolol took her hands out her pockets. You know what it is don't you, luv?

Dad: No, but I'm fascinated.

Mam: She don't want to work, her.

Dad: Ah, that'll be it then, luv.

Mam: She's got a new fella. She just wants to be gallavanting. She'll be back for a job once he's chucked her. She thinks he's going to take her and those two kids and they're not even his. He'll never leave his wife for her. They never do, do they?

Dad: No, but some of them must be very tempted.

FRONT DOOR SLAMS DOWNSTAIRS.

Mam: That's our Denise back.

MUFFLED SOUND OF DENISE SHRIEKING.

Sounds like Dave's with her.

MUFFLED SOUND OF DAVE AND DENISE ARGUING
THROUGH REST OF THIS SCENE.

I can't believe this time next week them two will be married.

Dad: Sounds like they're already married now.

Mam: You don't think they're having a row do you?

Denise: (SHOUTING AT DAVE DOWNSTAIRS) Get lost.

Mam: They are, they're having a row. Jim, they're having a right
go at it. It's much worse than last week.

Dad: Do you think you should pop down and have a word with
her?

Mam: (PUTTING SLIPPERS ON) I don't know whether I
should.

Antony: (SHOUTING FROM HIS ROOM) Shut it. We're trying
to kip up here.'

Mam: (CALLING TO ANTONY) You shut up, Antony. (TO
DAD) I think I might go down, Jim.

Dad: All right luv, you sort it out.

CUT TO:

Scene 2

<u>INT. NIGHT–LIVING ROOM</u>
(MAM, DAD, DAVE, DENISE)

Denise: (UPSET) If you think I'll marry you now, you pig. I'm not. A load of lads fancy me but I never bother with them.

Dave: Well bother with them if you want to.

Denise: I don't want to. Every time we see Beverly Macca it's the same. You love flirting with her. I saw your face, you love it.

Dave: I'm not even talking about this crap.

Denise: I could wear a low top like that and a bleeding mini-skirt but I've got more respect for myself, but you don't, you don't respect me.

MAM ENTERS AND COMFORTS DENISE WHO IS NOW IN TEARS.

Mam: Dave, what have you done now?

Dave: I've done nowt.

Mam: Well she's not crying over nothing is she?

Denise: He was flirting with Beverly Macca.

Dave: Was I hell . . . I'm a DJ, right . . . she was asking for a record.

Denise: Yeh, 'All right, darling' he kept saying to her. Why did you give her a kiss when she went?

Dave: She came over to me.

Denise: (GETTING EMOTIONAL) Every time I came out of the toilet she was round him like flies around shit and (TO DAVE) you're the shit and she's not even the fly cos she's too fat to be a fly, she's the shit as well, that's what you are, two shovels of shit . . . and that's it.

Mam: We don't have to bring shit into it.

Denise: Anyway that's it . . . you didn't even want to get married, every single time I mention it, you're not interested.

Dave: I'm sick of this, I'm going home.

Mam: Well you can't drive can you? You've had a drink.

Dave: I'm all right.

Mam: No, you're not all right. (CALLING UPSTAIRS) Jim!

Denise: No, let him go, Mam. Let him kill himself if that's what he wants.

Mam: Denise, you don't mean that.

Dave: Every time I do a gig round here we get this crap.

Denise: Yeh, every time you do a gig round here that cow is there.

DAD ARRIVES. HE IS IN HIS VEST AND PJ BOTTOMS.

Dad: What's going on here?

Mam: They're arguing over Beverly Macca.

Dad: She's all right here . . . tasty piece.

Mam: Jim!

Denise: I'm not getting married next Saturday.

Dad: That's a few bob saved . . . let's get back to bed.

Mam: Jim!

Dad: Look, this is just the ale talking, the pair of you are canned up.

Dave: I'm not canned up.

Dad: What were you drinking, bloody water?

Mam: (TO DAVE AND DENISE) It's a big step you're taking. You're bound to be feeling 'ett up. We're all fed up with the wedding. We've just got to grit our teeth and get on with it.

Denise: (GETTING EMOTIONAL AGAIN) I can't believe you said that. You're fed up, the happiest day of my life.

Mam: Let's all have a nice cup of tea.

Dad: I'll put kettle on.

DAD EXITS.

Denise: All I wanted was to have the happiest day of my life and just to live happy ever after . . . and he, Peter Stringfellow, he's (MEANING DAVE) spoilt it.

Mam: I know.

Dave: I'm going in there. It's doing my head in this.

Denise: He's more bothered about the stag night than the wedding.

Mam: Well you're having a hen night, aren't you?

Denise: Yeh . . . I'm going to have a brilliant time just to spite him . . . Get!

CUT TO:

Scene 3

<u>INT. NIGHT–KITCHEN</u>
(DAVE, DAD, ANTONY)

Dad: Just grin and bare it, cock, it'll all be over in a couple of weeks. Our Denise is just like her mother. Barbara always has a go at me when she's pissed . . . mind you, she has a go at me when she's sober an' all.

Dave: I'm looking forward to this wedding. Just cos I don't do a song and dance about it every two minutes . . .

ANTONY ENTERS WEARING BOXER SHORTS.

Antony: Is there any tea going? What's happening?

Dad: I don't know if you know, these two are getting married next week.

Antony: What is it this time?

Dave: Denise got a cob on cos I was talking to Beverly Macca that's the top and bottom of it.

Antony: She's got gorgeous knockers her.

Dave: I wouldn't know.

Dad: She has, son. Jesus, go and ask your mam where she's hid that whisky. We could all do with a drop in us tea.

Antony: Yeah, right. I love whisky me.

ANTONY EXITS.

Dave: You haven't got owt to eat have you?

Dad: Don't let Denise see you filling your face at a time like this. There's a bit of ham in there, shove it in a bloody butty.

ANTONY RETURNS.

Antony: It's in the pan cupboard, Dad.

Dad: Pan cupboard, bloody hell, she's not expecting burglars is she? Tell you what, you couldn't have a row every week, could you?

DAD GETS WHISKY OUT OF CUPBOARD AND POURS A BIT IN EACH CUP OF TEA.

Dave: (FISHING IN PANTRY) Is that beetroot going spare?

Dad: Get it down yer.

Antony: Are you making me one, Dave?

Dave: (PUTTING LAST BIT OF BEETROOT ON HIS BUTTY) None left.

Antony: Where's the Club biscuits?

DAD TAKES DRINKS THROUGH.

CUT TO:

Scene 4

INT. NIGHT–LIVING ROOM
(MAM, DAD, DENISE)

DAD ENTERS WITH DRINKS

Dad: There you go. Come on Denise . . . He's dead upset in there.

Denise: I don't care . . . is he?

Dad: He thinks the bloody world of you Denise. He's a good lad, Dave. He's a goodhearted bloody lad . . . always got his hand in his pocket at the club . . . not like his old fellow, Limp-a-Long Leslie. Come on, luv, try and drink it, I've put a bit of whisky in there for your nerves.

Mam: She doesn't need any more. She's pissed as it is.

Denise: I'm not pissed. I only had about nine, it's just too much for me the wedding and . . .him.

Dad: He's all right the big long streak of piss.

Denise: What's he doing in there?

Dad: He's just talking it over.

Denise: With Antony! He knows nowt.

Dad: Is there owt on? Put the telly on, Barbara.

Mam: No I'm not. That's why nothing gets sorted in this house. Nobody talks.

Dad: You do nothing but talk. You've bent my ear for the last hour, boring the arse off me about Pauline and her flexitime.

Mam: It was Donna! I knew you weren't listening. I don't know why I bother to keep our relationship going.

DAD IS PICKING HIS NOSE.

Denise: Dad, stop picking your nose.

Dad: How can you be bothered about me picking my nose with all the troubles you've got?

Mam: Haven't you got a hanky?

Dad: What, in my pyjamas? There's barely enough room for my tackle.

Mam: Do we need to know, Jim?

Dad: Is that it, kiddo? Is it all off then?

Denise: I don't know. I've got to have a think in my head.

Mam: Do you remember when Dave first came round? He never said a word for three months then he took that old armchair to the tip for us and it really broke the ice.

Dad: Bloody hell, you don't half talk some rubbish, Barbara.

Mam: Well it did.

Dad: Well he's better than that Stuart lad you went out with from the flats . . . he was a gormless get him, he couldn't find his arse with both hands.

Mam: Uh, I was happy when you broke that engagement off. (PAUSE) Do you remember when Dave came to Cleethorpes with us in that four-berth and he took his shoes off and nobody dared say owt?

Dad: I bloody did. They were rife. They wanted a stake through them.

Denise: They've gone a lot better now I've got him that stuff from the Avon.

Mam: You see, he does make an effort for you.

Dad: Ey kid . . . it don't mean nowt looking at someone's three-penny bits, you're only looking.

Denise: I know, Dad. It's just her, Beverly Macca, she just winds me up her . . . she's always laughing at everything he says with a big loud laugh . . . he's not that funny.

Dad: I know, luv, I know . . . (PAUSE) I'll tell you what, Barbara, don't give me rhubarb, it's repeating on me something shocking.

Mam: I've got some Gaviscon or some Rennies if you want.

Dad: I don't fancy either of them . . . you better get us a couple of Rennies.

MAM GOES INTO THE KITCHEN.

Dad: (QUIETLY) Listen Denise, don't worry gel, it'll be all right . . . them Rennies'll do the trick.

CUT TO:

Scene 5

<u>INT. NIGHT–KITCHEN</u>
(MAM, ANTONY, DAVE)

MAM ENTERS AND GOES OVER TO MEDICINE CUPBOARD. DAVE IS FINISHING EATING A LARGE SANDWICH. ANTONY IS EATING A KIT-KAT.

Mam: (TO ANTONY) Hey, gannet . . . them Kit-Kats are for your dad. (LOOKING IN CUPBOARD) Have you seen them Rennies?

Antony: I've not had them.

Mam: I didn't say you'd had them, I said have you seen them. It's a wonder you've not had them, you've had everything else. (MAM NOW LOOKING IN JUNK DRAWERS) Do you know, you can't find anything in this house. (FINDING THEM) Here they are. (TURNING TO GO) Are you coming in Dave?

Dave: Is she calmed down a bit?

Mam: Yeh, it's all blown over.

Dave: Barbara . . . there were nowt going on there, y'know.

Mam: I know Dave, it's that Beverly Macca.

TO LIVING ROOM.

CUT TO:

Scene 6

INT. NIGHT–LIVING ROOM
(MAM, DAD, DENISE, DAVE, ANTONY)

MAM, DAVE AND ANTONY ENTER. DAD AND DENISE ARE WATCHING TELLY. MAM GIVES DAD RENNIES.

Mam: Here y'are luv. Ah Jim, turn that telly off.

Dad: All right luv, it's only shite on at this time.

Antony: Is the *Equalizer* on?

Dad: *Equalizer* my arse. (TURNS IT OFF)

AN AWKWARD PAUSE WHERE DAD GIVES DAVE THE NOD
TO SAY SOMETHING.

Dave: (TO DENISE) Hey panda-eyes, they match that top.

Denise: I'm not laughing Dave . . . I'm still not speaking to you.

Dave: That's good. I thought I'd gone deaf.

Dad: Do you know, I feel lousy.

Mam: You've not given them Rennies a chance have you? You've
just shoved them in your mouth.

Dad: I think I've got liver failure.

Mam: Don't be so daft.

Dad: I've got a pain in my kidneys.

Mam: What, is it moving round your body?

Dad: Where are your kidneys?

DAD GROANS THROUGHOUT FOLLOWING DIALOGUE.

Mam: In your back. How can you have a pain in them if you
don't know where they are?

Denise: Remember last time when it was trapped wind?

Mam: You don't think it was them pork chops, do you.

Denise: We'd all have it, wouldn't we?

Mam: No, some people are funny with pork. Do you want me to get the doctor?

Dad: Oh no, there's no need for that.

Denise: He can't be that bad, can he.

Mam: He was right as rain when the football match was on.

Dave: Who won?

Dad: County, one–nil.

Dave: Yes! Who scored?

Dad: Hughes, header, fifty-sixth minute.

Dave: Magic.

Dad: Uh, I feel as weak as a bloody kitten.

Denise: Give us a fag, Dad, before you josh it.

Mam: You've probably just pulled something, Jim. Put a bit of Fiery Jack on it.

Denise: Uh no, I hate that stuff, it stinks the house out.

Dad: (HE MAKES A BIG BURP) I think that might have shifted it.

Mam: Told you it was heartburn. Uh, Jim, you had me worried there.

Dad: That's how it'll happen one day. You want to treat that as a dress-rehearsal. (BURP) I feel miles better for that. (TO DENISE) Now, are you two getting married or not?

Mam: Course they are, aren't you?

Denise: I don't know – what do you think, Dave?

Dave: Might as well.

Denise: All right, seen as you've apologized to me.

Dad: Right . . . Antony, make us another drink, we're celebrating now.

Antony: We've just had one.

Dad: Yeh, but I was dying then, I couldn't enjoy it.

Mam: I'm glad I didn't call that doctor. I wouldn't know where to put my face. We'll have a brew and then we'll get off to bed and Denise, you'll have to get that sleeping-bag out of the airing-cupboard for Dave.

ANTONY GOES TO MAKE A BREW.

I didn't tell you, Nana rang . . . she wants us to look after Robson. She's going to see Auntie Annie.

Dad: Can't she take it with her?

Mam: Not to Blackpool . . . anyway, Annie's got a cat.

Denise: It's crap that budgie, it can't even talk.

Dad: Oh, it can talk . . . it's just you're nana won't let it get a word in edgeways.

Mam: It doesn't hardly even squawk now since Jerome died . . . they were in love those two.

Dave: They're two blokes, Robson and Jerome.

Mam: I know, but it's only names . . . you couldn't tell which was the boy and which was the girl.

Dad: I bet they could.

Mam: Anyway, budgies are blind.

Dad: Are they buggery . . . how the hell are they going to find their perch? . . . They'd be on their arse in the bottom of the cage all the time.

Mam: Oh, that's bats I'm thinking of.

Dave: A mate of mine used to work in a pet shop you know, but he got sacked . . .

Mam: Oh, why?

Dave: Caught him with his hand in the Trill. (IN TRIUMPH) Yes . . . the old ones are the best.

DAD LAUGHS LONG AND LOUD.

Mam: You daft pair of beggars.

ANTONY ENTERS WITH TEA.

Dad: Hey flash, forget the tea, just bring the whisky.

Mam: Look at him now, I'm glad I didn't call that doctor.

Denise: Ey Dave, do my dad that impression of Paul Daniels you do.

Dave: No, go 'way.

Denise: Go on.

Mam: Go on Dave, I love impressions.

Dave: No.

Mam: No, go on.

Antony: Who's he doing?

Dave: That's magic.

ONLY DENISE LAUGHS.

Antony: That's Orville that.

Dad: Rory Bremner's job's safe isn't it.

Dave: Hey, remember that time they had Paul Daniels on *Spitting Image* in bed with Debbie. He was balancing a glass of milk on his head and he whipped his rug off from under it and the milk stays on his head . . . (LAUGHS) . . . THAT WAS TOP THAT.

DAVE AND DENISE LAUGH.

Dad: You're a bit simple you two.

Mam: Is that that thing with puppets? I never got that me. I don't like puppets me.

Dad: You like the *Muppets*.

Mam: Yes, I like the *Muppets*.

Dad: Barbara, it's time for bed, luv.

Denise: Uh, it's freezing in here, can we put the fire on.

Dad: No need for that, we're going to bed after this drink.

Mam: If you're not warm enough in that sleeping-bag there's blankets in the airing-cupboard.

Dad: They're made for Arctic conditions them sleeping-bags.

Denise: Just as well in here.

Dad: When I was courting your mam, I couldn't stay over then, no matter how cold it was I had to walk home.

Mam: Well, you didn't have a car did you?

Dad: Well.

Mam: I am glad that wedding's back on again. I'm always upset when you call it off.

Dad: To the wedding. How long have we been together Barb?

Mam: Twenty-seven years.

Dad: Twenty-seven years, Dave, and never a cross word.

MAM GIVES HIM A LOOK.

Mam: Jim, what are you on about?

Dad: (SINGS) How to handle a woman . . . is to love her . . . simply love her.

EVERYBODY LAUGHS.

Mam: You big soft aper, you haven't a clue have you?

Dad: I missed my way there . . . I was the Mick Hucknall of our estate in my day you know.

Denise: Dad, sing that one for Dave that you used to sing to Ant when he was a little baby.

Antony: Oh no.

Dad: (SINGS GIVING IT LOADS OF ACTING) Walking down the street in ragged clothes is not a joke,
People laugh at me and call me beggar cos I'm broke,
But there's one little lad and he calls me Dad,
Shake hands with a millionaire.

ALL CLAP AND CHEER.

Dad: Ey Ant, go and get me that banjo.

Mam: Oh bugger off Jim, it's one o'clock in the morning.

Dad: Go on I'm enjoying myself . . . we're twenty-four-hour party people us.

Antony: Go on, Mam, let him.

Denise: Go on, Mam.

Mam: All right then, I thought I'd seen the back of that.

ANTONY GOES IN THE HALL TO GET IT AND RUSHES STRAIGHT BACK.

Dad: Have you heard me on the banjo, Dave?

Dave: Yeh, I have . . . several times.

Antony: I thought I was getting that.

Dad: That's very nice of you son. Following in your father's musical footsteps.

Antony: Get a few bob for that down the car boot.

DAD DOES A QUICK TUNE-UP THEN STRAIGHT INTO A MUSICAL NUMBER, 'I WANNA GIRL'. EVERYONE CLAPS AND CHEERS AT THE END.

Dad: Right, any requests?

Mam: Yes, let's get to bed.

Denise: You give us a song, Mam.

Mam: No, it's one o'clock in the morning.

Dad: Go on, Barbara, you're not going on at the Palladium.

All (EXCEPT MAM): (CHANTING) Barbara, Barbara, Barbara.

Mam: I don't remember any songs.

Denise: What's that one you sing when you're washing up? . . . Or shall I sing.

Dave: Oh no!

Dad: Uh Barbara, quick bail us out, luv . . . remember when she was pissed at the Feathers doing her Whitney Houston . . . even the landlord complained.

MAM SINGS 'YOU WERE MADE FOR ME'. ALL LAUGH AS SHE ENDS THE FIRST LINE. MAM CONTINUES BUT IS SINGING A LITTLE FLAT . . . DURING THIS THE REST OF

THE FAMILY HOLD THEIR SIDES TRYING NOT TO LAUGH.
MAM POINTS AT THEM STERNLY AND CARRIES ON. AS
SHE FINISHES THEY ALL CHEER.

Denise: Ant, do that muscle-man thing.

Dad: That reminds me, any chicken left.

Antony: What are we going to sing now?

Mam: Come on that's it, time for bed.

Dad: Don't be a bloody killjoy, I was going to put one bar of the
fire on.

Mam: Here Antony, go and hide that thing. (CALLING AFTER
HIM) And get that sleeping-bag for Dave while you're there.

Denise: Hey Dad, will you play the banjo at our reception.

Dad: Oh aye, it's all paid for your reception. We'll have a bloody
good time even if it kills us.

ANTONY COMES BACK IN WITH SLEEPING-BAG.

Antony: I'm going to bed.

Denise: Goodnight muscle-man.

ANTONY EXITS.

Mam: Will that be warm enough for you, Dave?

Dave: Yeh, sound that, Barbara.

Mam: There's no pillows for you.

Dave: I'll be all right, I'll put a couple of cushions together.

Mam: Yeh, put a couple of cushions together.

Dad: Goodnight.

Mam: Shall I leave that big light for you, love?

Dad: Will you buggery, he'll forget to put it off. C'mon Denise.

MAM AND DAD EXIT.

Denise: Night Casanova.

Dave: (JOKING) Night Bev . . . Uh, Denise.

Denise: Don't push it.

DENISE EXITS. DAVE GETS UNDRESSED SINGING 'YOU WERE MADE FOR ME'. HE GETS INTO BED. DENISE ENTERS IN HER DRESSING GOWN.

Denise: Dave, I love you, y'big pillock.

Dave: Come and give us a cuddle.

Denise: Have you farted?

END OF EPISODE.

Episode 6

Scene 1

<u>INT. MORNING–BEDROOM</u>
(MAM, DENISE, CHERYL, NANA)

DENISE IS SITTING AT DRESSING TABLE MESSING WITH HER HAIR. SHE IS IN A NIGHTGOWN. CHERYL IS IN HER BRIDESMAID DRESS. MAM IS IN A SMART TWO-PIECE OUTFIT.

Mam: Stop messing with your hair, Denise, she's done it lovely.

Denise: Is it too Princess Ann?

All: No.

Denise: I wanted a load of bits all coming down round my face.

Mam: It'll all be coming down round your face if you're not careful.

Denise: You know what I want, don't you Cheryl? She's shite that Sandra Beswick. She weren't interested, were she Mam?

Mam: She was definitely hungover.

Nana: (CALLING FROM DOWNSTAIRS) Anyone want a sandwich?

Mam: (CALLING BACK) No.

Nana: (CALLING FROM DOWNSTAIRS) I'm doing myself one, is that all right Barbara?

Mam: (CALLING BACK) Yeh. (THEN TO DENISE) I don't know what she's filling her face for at this time. She's got all day to fill her face.

Cheryl: Have you had any breakfast, Denise?

Denise: I've not been able to get owt down, have I Mam? I've got butterflies like you wouldn't believe. (HOLDING OUT SHAKY HAND) Look at that. (PAUSE) You look gorgeous Cheryl, doesn't she Mam?

Mam: You look like a china doll.

Cheryl: I'll tell you what . . . it's pinching me under the arms this, it's really tight.

Denise: Is it heck. You look gorgeous an' all Mam . . . doesn't she Cheryl? That suit.

Mam: Well I had to get something good. Dave's mam's suit is from Marks's . . . can't let the side down, can I?

Denise: Now look at me. Come 'ere, be honest – is that too much blusher?

Mam: You can't have too much blusher on your wedding day.

Cheryl: Well, you're the blushing bride aren't you. (LAUGHS)

Denise: Light us a fag, Cheryl.

Mam: Light us one an'all, will you. Thanks luv. I'm a bag of nerves . . . shall we have a drop of brandy.

Denise: Uh, I don't want to stink of booze today. Uh, go on then, just a little one.

Mam: I don't see why, they're all in the Feathers.

MAM EXITS.

Denise: Ey Cheryl, pull us a bit more of this down.

Cheryl: Oh Denise, you'll look like the bloody Dulux dog.

CUT TO:

Scene 2

INT. MORNING–KITCHEN
(MAM, NANA, DAVE, DAD, TWIGGY, CHERYL)

NANA IS MAKING A SANDWICH. MAM ENTERS.

Mam: Are you all right, Mam?

Nana: Don't worry about me, I'll see to myself. Have you got a bit of Piccalilly for this cheese? I couldn't see any. I didn't like to root on the wedding day.

Mam: Ere'ya, you'll have to put it on yourself.

Nana: It's Gwen's husband's funeral on Monday ... I said to Gwen ... So it's a wedding on the Saturday and a funeral on the Monday. I'd like to wear these new shoes, because they'll be wore in by then ... but I'm not wearing this outfit, it's a bit too jazzy for a funeral.

Mam: Oh, you don't want to wear that outfit, Mam.

TWIGGY ENTERS FROM OUTSIDE DRESSED FOR THE WEDDING BUT LOOKING SLIGHTLY WORSE FOR DRINK.

Twiggy: Barbara . . . the state of Dave! Here you are lad, c'mon.

DAD HELPS DAVE IN. BOTH LOOK PARALYTIC.

Mam: Jim! How could you let this happen?

DAVE, DAD AND TWIGGY SOBER UP AND CELEBRATE THEIR FANTASTIC JOKE.

Dad: Ah, reel her in . . . we're having you on, cock.

Dave/Dad/Twiggy: (SING) Here we go, here we go, here we go.

Mam: Uh, you shower of shite . . . it's not funny that.

Nana: (UNPHASED) Barbara, there's no Piccalilly left in this jar.

Mam: Oh shut up Mother.

Dad: All right Norma . . . when are you getting changed, luv?

Nana: Get lost . . . I've not got my hat on yet.

Dad: Uh, that'll be a belter . . . have you borrowed Cilla's?

Mam: Dave, what are you doing here? If Denise comes down, the wedding'll be off.

Dave: What do you think I've come for? (LAUGHS) . . . I'm just on my way back from the pub.

Mam: Well it's unlucky to see the bride on the morning of the wedding.

Dad: I can't remember seeing you before.

DAD LAUGHS AND DAVE AND TWIGGY JOIN IN.

Mam: Sod off the lot of you . . . You're a waste of time the lot of you. Jim, get him out of here, pronto.

MAM EXITS TO STAIRS.

Nana: (TO DAVE) Do you want a sandwich, luv?

Dave: No thanks, Nana.

Nana: There's not much Piccalilly left.

Dad: (TO DAVE) Do you think we can carry on with the celebrations in the light of that revelation?

Dave: (CARRYING ON THE JOKE) I don't know, Jim . . . tricky that.

Twiggy: I'll tell you what . . . you're looking lovelier than ever.

Nana: Get off.

Twiggy: I'll tell you what, you'll be snapped up at that wedding.

Nana: I hope so.

Dad: Do you want a trowel . . . if you're going to lay it on any thicker. Are we having a drop of brandy?

Nana: Barbara's took that upstairs.

Dad: No problem, a nice little drop of whisky?

Twiggy: Oh aye, go down a treat with mi sarni that.

Dad: Do you want some, Norma?

Nana: Well, I only usually have a sherry at Christmas . . . my stout of an evening . . .

Dad: (INTERRUPTING STERNLY) Yes or no?

Nana: Yes.

Dad: Just say so . . . (STRAIGHTENING UP TO TOAST) To my little girl Denise and her . . .

Dave: Hang on, Jim . . . it's not your speech yet.

Dad: Oh no, cock . . . you'll know when it is . . . I've put a few jokes in.

Nana: It's not blue is it, Jim?

Dad: No, sorry luv . . . you'll have to watch your Chubby Brown videos for that.

Twiggy: I love Chubby Brown. I saw him last year at the Apollo . . . he was absolutely disgusting . . . bloody marvellous . . . you'd have loved him, Norma.

Nana: I don't like anything blue me.

Twiggy: No you're like me there, girl.

Nana: Will one of you big fellas put the film in my camera? I've got a thirty-six 'cos it's going to be a long day in't it?

CHERYL ENTERS. DAVE WOLF-WHISTLES.

Dad: Ey up, gorgeous.

Twiggy: Drop 'em, blossom . . . sorry, Norma . . . it's only a compliment.

Dad: Ey up, Dave, if Denise don't turn up, you could always marry Cheryl in that rig out.

Cheryl: Denise is dead mad with you, Dave. She wants you out of here. She says you're jeopardizing your future happiness together.

Dave: I'm going off in a minute. Ey, did she like her flowers?

Cheryl: Yeh, they're gorgeous them. Where did you get them from?

Dave: I don't know. Where did you get them from, Twiggy?

Twiggy: If you knew that you'd know as much as me kid.

Dave: (TO CHERYL) She all right?

Cheryl: She's starting to panic.

Dave: Tell her she's not the only one . . . my arse is like that. (DOING HAND GESTURE)

CHERYL EXITS.

Nana: Where's your best man? Barry is it?

Dave: No Gary . . . he's got to work. He couldn't get the morning off. He's going straight from the butchers.

Dad: That's all we want, church stinking of bloody mince.

Twiggy: Hey, watch what will happen . . . he'll put his hand in his pocket for the ring and pull out a pork chop! (LAUGHS)

CUT TO:

Scene 3

<u>INT. MORNING–BEDROOM</u>
(DENISE, MAM, CHERYL, NANA)

Denise: (CRYING) I hate my hair, he's downstairs, it's all going wrong.

Mam: Never mind, luv . . . it's all too much, in't it?

Denise: What's he doing down there?

Cheryl: He's just with your dad and Twiggy. He says his arse is like that.

Mam/Denise: Ah!

Denise: Does he look nice in his suit?

Cheryl: Uh yeh, gorgeous . . . Ey, I think Twiggy's trying to cop with me.

Denise: You wouldn't go with him, would you?

Cheryl: No . . . Twiggy! No way.

Denise: You would, wouldn't you.

Cheryl: Yeh, I would.

NANA ENTERS PUFFING AND PANTING.

Mam: Are you all right, Mam?

Nana: I can't be doing with them stairs, Barbara. Where's the bride-to-be?

Denise: Hiya Nana.

Nana: Ah how are you, luv?

Denise: Nana.

DENISE STILL LOOKS LIKE SHE'S BEEN CRYING.

Nana: This is the happiest day of your life this, luv . . . it all goes downhill from here, doesn't it, Barbara?

Mam: Oh leave it, Mam.

Nana: (TO DENISE) I've brought you them earrings up.

Denise: Thank you.

Nana: Here y'are.

Mam: Now are these something old or something borrowed?

Nana: Borrowed. I'm sorry, luv, I couldn't part with them . . . even for you.

Mam: (TAKING OFF NECKLACE AND GIVING TO DENISE) Here, have this then.

Denise: Your heart necklace, for keeps? Cheryl, look.

Nana: What's your something blue?

Denise: Cheryl got me this garter.

DENISE SHOWS GARTER.

Mam: Kinky.

Nana: If I get married again, the something blue would be the veins down me leg. (LAUGHS)

Mam: Do you want a brandy, Mam?

Nana: No, you know me, I don't like to drink.

Mam: Just a small one then.

Nana: Go on then, just to wet my whistle. Make it a double while you're at it. (PAUSE) That was a lovely bit of cheese that Barbara, where did you get it?

Mam: In the precinct. I can't believe the day's finally come . . . we seemed to have been planning it for ages. (REMEMBERING)

Denise: Well we were. What time is it?

Mam: Oh, it's ten past.

Denise: Mam, will you go and get rid of that nobhead I'm marrying . . . it's doing my head in, this.

CUT TO:

Scene 4A

INT. MORNING–KITCHEN
(DAD, DAVE, MAM, TWIGGY, ANTONY)

ANTONY HAS HAD A SHARP HAIRCUT AND IS BEING RIDICULED.

Dad: Have you had your hair cut or your ears lowered?

EVERYONE APART FROM ANTONY LAUGHS.

Twiggy: Tell me who they were and I'll get them. (LAUGHS)

Dave: Ohh, that must smart. Looks like they cut that from the inside.

MAM ENTERS.

Mam: Oh Antony, you look lovely. Take no notice of this scruffy lot. You've got five minutes . . . get upstairs and get that suit on. It's layed out on your bed.

ANTONY EXITS.

And you Dave . . . you better go.

Dave: I was just going.

Twiggy: Hang on, I'm just going for a slash.

TWIGGY EXITS.

Mam: Uh, I better go and do my mam's hat. It's all go. I don't know whether I'm coming or going.

MAM EXITS.

Dad: (TO DAVE) All right, kiddo?

Dave: Yeh.

Dad: Not long now. I'll give you same advice my old dad gave me years ago on my wedding day. (BECOMING SECRETIVE IN HIS MANNER) A little tip. To keep 'em sweet. Listen . . . whenever you're going out on a night and you know you're going to be back at half eleven, tell 'em you're going to be back at twelve.

Then, when you come in at eleven thirty, you're in their good books, see. They think you've come home early for them . . . you know what I'm saying. Always stay one step ahead.

Dave: Ey, good one that, Jim.

Dad: Aye, up there for thinking, down there for dancing.

Dave: Anyway, I better go an't I? I'll see you later won't I?

Dad: Ey son, you will look after her won't you?

Dave: Aye Jim, I will.

CUT TO:

Scene 4B

INT. MORNING–BEDROOM
(CHERYL, TWIGGY, DENISE)

TWIGGY KNOCKS ON THE BEDROOM DOOR. DENISE IS NOW MADE-UP BUT IS STILL IN HER DRESSING GOWN.

Twiggy: Hey Norma, no sliding down the bannister, girl. Are you decent?

Denise: Yeh.

Twiggy: Ah, I'll come in anyway. (LAUGHS) Hey Denise, you look lovely.

Denise: It's only me dressing gown.

Twiggy: I know but if you look that good in a dressing gown . . . Hey, this is your last chance . . . I've got a fast car downstairs . . .

two tickets to Rio in the glovebox and a load of knock-off sports gear in the boot . . . what do you say?

Denise: Ah, you're tempting me now, Twiggy.

Cheryl: What sort of sports gear you got?

Twiggy: Well I've got a load of tracky bottoms, I'm getting them out at the reception. I'll sort you out.

Denise: Hey, how's Dave?

Twiggy: I'm not sure that he isn't having second thoughts but he's got a lovely suit on but he's wearing a pair of running shoes.

Denise: Don't Twiggy, I'm a bag of nerves. Imagine what a state I'd look if he didn't turn up.

Twiggy: Hey, but imagine what a state he'd look when you'd caught him. He's skipping off nowhere. I'll break his legs for you if I have to.

Denise: Ah, cheers Twiggy.

Twiggy: Have a great day. See you, kiddo.

TWIGGY EXITS.

Denise: Ah, heart of gold him in't he?

Cheryl: To be honest if there's no one better . . . I'm going to cop with him tonight.

Denise: Ah . . . he'd be made up with that.

CUT TO:

Scene 4C

INT. MORNING–KITCHEN
(DAD, DAVE, TWIGGY, JOE, MARY)

DAD AND DAVE DRINKING. TWIGGY ENTERS.

Twiggy: Hey Dave, I just popped my head round. She's far too good for you, you ugly get. Come on, mucker. (JOKING TO DAD) I'll make sure he doesn't do a runner.

Dad: See ya son, see ya Twiggy.

DAD STANDS A MINUTE ON HIS OWN. HE TAKES OUT SCRIPT AND MIMES AND MOUTHS HIS SPEECH, LEADING THE LAUGHTER AT THE JOKES. JOE ENTERS, CATCHING DAD BY SURPRISE.

Dad: All right Joe?

Joe: Yeh.

Dad: Just going through my speech.

Joe: Right.

Dad: You've got to walk a fine line you know, what with Dave's family being there, don't want to be too blue.

Joe: No. (PAUSE) Shame.

Dad: Yeh. (PAUSE) Your Cheryl looks smart in the dress, doesn't she?

Joe: Aye, she does. (PAUSE) It's cutting her under the arms.

Dad: What?

Joe: The dress. She's too fat for it.

MARY ENTERS.

Mary: Oh Jim, it's the big day. I'm as nervous as if it were my own.

Dad: You look lovely, kid, you look like one of them leprechauns.

Mary: Thanks Jim. It's only C&A. You look lovely yourself, Jim. Do you like Joe's suit there? He bought it for his brother's funeral.

Joe: Aye, fifty-two he was.

AWKWARD PAUSE AS DAD STRUGGLES WITH WHAT TO SAY.

CUT TO:

Scene 5

INT. MORNING–LIVING ROOM
(DAD, MAM, NANA, JOE, MARY, ANTONY, DENISE, CHERYL)

MAM IS HELPING NANA PUT ON HER HAT. ANTONY IS SHINING HIS SHOES WHILST WATCHING MOTOR RACING ON TV. DAD, MARY AND JOE ENTER.

Mam: Mam said it was too far forward before. Leave it there . . . that's the fashionable way to wear these.

Mary: Hiya everyone.

Mam: Hiya Mary.

Mary: Ooh Barbara, can you believe it?

Mam: I know, it's chaos in here. Denise was crying earlier. It's all right, Cheryl's with her now, they're having a bitch about Beverly Macca.

Mary: Oh, that's good.

Mam: Antony . . . turn that thing down. What are you doing, cleaning your shoes in here like that? Get a newspaper down.

ANTONY GETS NEWSPAPER AND LAYS IT AT THE FOOT OF HIS CHAIR. HE TURNS THE TV DOWN A NOTCH.

Dad: Who wants a whisky?

Mary: Uh, not for me Jim.

Dad: Joe?

Joe: Ta.

Mam: Antony, I won't tell you again . . . turn it down!

Antony: I've just turned it.

Mam: Well turn it again.

ANTONY TURNS TV VOLUME DOWN FURTHER.

Dad: (POURING DRINK) Barbara?

Mam: Just a little one, luv.

Dad: Norma?

Nana: Yes please.

Antony: Can I have one, Dad?

Dad: No.

Mary: Oh, look at Antony's lovely haircut. You look like a little choirboy.

Dad: He looks like a little gay boy.

Mam: You know, I've been so busy this morning I've hardly smoked. (TO DAD) Give us one now.

CHERYL ENTERS.

Cheryl: Are you ready? . . . Here comes the bride.

DAD LEADS EVERYONE TO SING THE TUNE OF 'HERE COMES THE BRIDE'. DENISE ENTERS. SHE'S NOW GOT HER VEIL ON AND CARRIES A DOLLY BAG. LOTS OF 'AHHHS'.

Mary: Isn't she lovely!

Denise: Does my hair look like shite?

Mary: No, you look gorgeous. Oh Jim, you must be proud. Oh, look at the pair of you . . . Denise the blushing bride, our Cheryl in dusky peach.

Antony: Ey Denise, you look dead nice in that dress, honest.

Denise: Cheers Ant . . . you don't look too bad yourself.

Nana: Them earrings set it off a treat, Denise.

Denise: Thanks Nana.

Nana: Don't lose them.

Dad: 'An't she got enough to worry about?

Denise: Dad, giz a ciggi . . . calm my nerves.

Dad: Take your time.

Joe: Denise.

Denise: Hiya Joe.

Joe: Nice outfit.

Denise: Thanks Joe.

Dad: Steady on Joe . . . you silver-tongued charmer.

Denise: It's me last day here. Will you miss us, Ant?

Antony: Yeh, like a hole in a parachute. I'm having your room.

Denise: Get lost, that's my room. What if me and Dave want to stop over?

Dad: You only live round the corner.

Denise: Mam, tell 'em.

Mam: We'll talk about it later. Now don't forget . . . ring in luv, when you get to Tenerife . . . let us know how you're going.

Dad: It'll be the middle of the night!

Antony: I'm having that room, I don't care.

Mary: We better get off, Barbara . . . our taxi'll be here in a minute . . . (TO DENISE) all the very best . . . (KISSES DENISE) we'll see you in church. (SINGS) 'Going to the Chapel and you're going to get married' (STOPS SINGING) It'll be a really lovely day I know it and there's lovely weather. God's smiling down on you already. Bye love.

Denise: Eh Mary, ta for making the dress.

Mary: Try to stand straight, Cheryl. That's a good girl.

Joe: (KISSING DENISE) See you later.

All: (AS JOE AND MARY EXIT) Bye.

Dad: Right . . . I'm going to have a quick Tom Tit.

Mam: Thanks for keeping us informed, Jim.

DAD EXITS UPSTAIRS.

Nana: He's lucky to be so regular. When you get to my age it's all or nothing.

Mam: What time are the cars coming?

Denise: I've just thought of something. Do you know what we've not thought about . . . how we're going to get all the presents back . . . we'll have to give you the keys to our flat cos we're not going back there . . . we're going straight to Tenerife.

CHERYL STARTS PAINTING DENISE'S NAILS.

You're best not leaving presents in that flat for a week – they'll get robbed . . . we'll bring them here and put them in your room.

Antony: No, I'm having her room . . . you can put them in my room.

DENISE MOVES, SMUDGING NAILS.

Denise: (NEEDING TO PLACE BLAME) Antony! Will you shut up about my room, look you've made Cheryl smudge my wedding nails.

Nana: You should have done them nails before you put the frock on . . . if that bottle goes over . . . that'll be it.

Mam: Antony, turn that off now . . . it's an important day.

Antony: I'm watching it.

Mam: No you're not, turn it off!

Denise: Blow on that, Cheryl.

DENISE BLOWS ON NAILS.

Nana: Cheryl, that looks tight on you that dress.

Cheryl: It's the style of dress.

MAM GIVES NANA DAGGERS. DAD ENTERS.

Dad: Uh Barbara, I'm shitting like a new-born baby.

Mam: It's just like you to have the runs on a day like today.

DAD EXITS TO KITCHEN.

Nana: It's not like that with me. I'm the other way. I thought today might have seen some movement . . . but no.

Cheryl: So Barbara, will I bring the presents back in my cab?

Dad: (CALLING FROM OTHER ROOM) Barbara . . . what have we got?

Mam: (CALLING BACK) We've got nothing. (THEN CALMLY TO CHERYL) Thanks Cheryl. I'll give you something towards the fare.

DAD RE-ENTERS GROANING.

Nana: Tell you what I'm thinking, Barbara, I'm going to get Dave to nip me home after the church do for my comfortable shoes . . . for the night-time do.

Denise: Dave won't be nipping you home, Nana.

Nana: He will. He thinks a lot about me does David.

Dad: He's the bleeding groom, Norma . . . he's not nipping no one nowhere, no how.

Denise: You'll have to ask someone else, Nana.

Nana: I don't like to ask anybody else.

Denise: But you don't mind asking the groom . . . Mam, tell her.

Mam: Mam, you'll have to get a taxi.

Nana: Uh no, no, them shoes are upstairs . . . it'll cost me a fortune.

ANTONY IS WATCHING THE TV WITH THE SOUND DOWN.

Dad: Ant, go and see if the chemist is open.

Antony: There's no time, we're off in a minute.

Dad: There's no time for watching telly then.

Mam: Why don't you stop off at the chemists on your way, Jim?

Denise: He's not stopping off at a bloody chemist whilst I'm sat there in my bride's dress like a nobhead. I'm a bag of nerves now.

Dad: I'll show you nerves on the back of the khazi if you want.

Mam: Right, that's it ... Antony, nip over the road ... see if Lorraine's got anything. Go on, shift yourself.

ANTONY EXITS.

Dad: Uh, we'll have to be quick going down that aisle if this keeps up.

Nana: I should have actually known not to wear new shoes ... Uh, I can't remember whether I've fed Robson now.

Dad: I'm sorry Denise ... the last thing I wanted was to be stood at the altar with you with ring-sting. I'll tell you what, if they pass that collection box round, it won't be money I'll be putting in it.

DAD EXITS.

Nana: So what are you going to do, Barbara?

Mam: About what?

Nana: About my shoes.

Mam: We've sorted that you're going to get a taxi.

Nana: Oh heck.

Denise: Don't forget, we've got to bring back the rest of that cake.

Cheryl: Shall I bring that in the taxi with me?

MAM LOOKS AT DAD IN A MOMENT OF HESITATION.

Mam: Yes, thanks Cheryl, luv.

ANTONY ENTERS.

Antony: She's not in . . . but taxi's here.

Nana: Oh, where's my bag?

Mam: Right, come on . . . Cheryl pass my mam her bag will you . . .

Antony: (GOING TOWARDS THE DOOR) I'm getting in the front.

Mam: Antony, come back and wish your sister good luck. It's the last time you'll see her as a single woman.

Antony: Good luck, fat arse.

Mam: Right, go and get in that taxi . . . that's as much as you'll get out of him.

Nana: Uh, good luck, Denise. (KISSES DENISE) I've got thirty-six films in my camera so I'm sure to get a good un.

Denise: Thanks Nana.

Cheryl: Do you want me to have your ciggies?

Denise: No, I'll shuv 'em in here. (PUTTING THEM IN DOLLY BAG)

CHERYL KISSES DENISE.

Cheryl: See you later, Mrs Best.

Denise: Tra . . . Ey Cheryl, I'll make sure you catch my posey.

Mam: Oh Denise, you look absolutely gorgeous. I just hope you'll be happy. He's a lovely lad, Dave . . . uh, little Denise, look at you.

DAD ENTERS ADJUSTING HIS PANTS.

Dad: I think I'm through the worst of it.

Mam: See you later, Jim.

MAM EXITS. DAD WALKS OVER TO THE WINDOW.

Dad: Ey, come and see your nana. Bloody hell, who else would get in a taxi arse first like that?

DENISE COMES OVER AND LOOKS OUT OF THE WINDOW.

Dad: Y'mam looks good, doesn't she . . . she's done you proud there . . . and Antony, he scrubbed up all right. What's up, cock?

Denise: (WELLING UP) Nothing . . . it's just the last time I'll be Denise Royle . . . it's dead weird getting married . . . I just hope I like it.

Dad: Ahh Denise, you'll love it. Do you know, you look radiant. You look like a little princess. I'm dead proud of you.

Denise: Even though I never kept down a job?

Dad: That doesn't matter now, luv . . . Let the other silly bugger do it . . .

DOORBELL RINGS.

Dad: (LOOKING OUT OF WINDOW) Ey, look at that . . . car . . . shame we're only going as far as the church in it.

DAD GOES TO FRONT DOOR.

Denise: Tell them I'm not ready yet. (DENISE WIPES HER EYES)

Dad (OOV): (SHOUTING TO DRIVER) Won't be a minute, pal, just a few last-minute preparations. (COMING BACK IN) Preparations my arse. (POURING WHISKY) Let's have a drop of whisky. (PASSING CIGARETTE) Ey Kid . . . have a ciggie off your old dad.

THEY BOTH LIGHT UP.

She does look a sight in that bridesmaid dress, doesn't she, Cheryl. (JOKING) Mind you, makes you look a damn-sight better in the photos.

Denise: Dad! Y'know, Dad, I never say anything nice to you. I'm always going on at you for picking your nose and farting . . .

Dad: I know luv.

Denise: You and m'mam . . . more than anything.

Dad: I know. Here kid. (OFFERING TOAST) To You!

BOTH CLICK GLASSES AND DOWN THE DRINK IN ONE.

Dad: (LEAVING) Uhh, I hope my arse holds up.

DAD EXITS. DENISE HESITATES AND LOOKS BACK AT ROOM, THEN EXITS.

END OF EPISODE.

What the Reviews said

Till scriptwriters us do part
Nancy Banks-Smith

. . . Which brings us to the last episode of *The Royle Family*, Denise's wedding. This, like the series itself, was quite unique as nothing whatsoever happened. Unless you count Jim's diarrhoea and Nana's constipation, which cancelled each other out.

At first the family are like looking at mould through a microscope. Then, irresistibly, they grow on you.

In their last moments together, Denise turned her vacant, flower-like face to her father and said, 'Dad, I know I never say anything nice to you. I'm always going on at you for picking your nose and farting. Well, you know I . . . you and me mam . . . both of you. More than anything.' It was as if a peach was struggling with the concept of speech. Striking acting from the clever Caroline Aherne.

There was a touching sense of tenderness, like a family of primates grooming each other in the Manchester rain forest. Just the eructation of the silverback male and Sir David, breathless in the bushes.

Guardian, 20 October 1998

The Royle Family

Comedy doesn't get less regal or more real-life than this series about a Manchester working-class family – 'typical' only in that its assemblage of warts-and-all comic characters draws on every

Mancunian cliché in the book. That, of course, is precisely the point for the team behind *Mrs Merton*, which specializes in manipulating everyday banalities to ironic effect. Sitting around a television, talking and bickering about who had what for tea, who has the best feet in the family, or who made a costly phone call to Aberdeen may not sound like a recipe for hilarity – but as nuanced by Ricky Tomlinson, Sue Johnston and Caroline Aherne, virtually every word has comic potential.

Telegraph, 14 September 1998

Watching television: it's the real thing
Nicholas Barber

There wasn't much of a fanfare to herald *The Royle Family*, but what little advance publicity there was described it as a comedy drama. You can only feel sorry for anyone who regards it as dramatic. 'Gasp . . . as Jim tries on a new pair of jeans! Scream . . . as Antony pours a cup of tea! Hide Behind The Sofa . . . as the family refuse to budge from theirs!' It is quite possibly the least dramatic programme ever made. A working class Mancunian family chain-smoke in front of the television, the neighbours pop in, and that's it. There are no scene changes. Half an hour of screen time is half an hour in the life of the Royles. *Seinfield* misleadingly labelled itself 'a show about nothing', when each episode was actually a Bayeux Tapestry of plot strands. *The Royle Family* is the real thing.

It's a high risk experiment to produce a series that has less plot than a dictionary, and the only way to succeed is to have some extraordinary dialogue. *The Royle Family* does. Caroline Aherne (or 'TV's Mrs Merton', in *OK! Magazine* parlance) stars as 26-year-old Denise, and she co-writes the programme with Henry Normal and Craig Cash, who appears as her fiancé, Dave. Antony (Ralf Little) is her surly 15-year-old brother. He grumbles when he is dispatched to the off-licence to replenish the family's cigarette supplies (he's not allowed to have any for himself until he's old enough to buy them legally), but, refreshingly, he can't be bothered to rebel against his parents. They are played by Ricky Tomlinson and Sue Johnston – Mr and Mrs Grant in *Brookside* – and they are terrific.

Tomlinson's Jim Royle, the archetypal miserable sod, picks a nose like a rotting strawberry in between delivering the best lines. He hears that Dave's dad is on a disability allowance, so won't be chipping in for the forthcoming wedding, and he is exasperated by this injustice: 'He's paying bugger all, and he'll get a better parking space!' If this doesn't seem hilarious in print, then I promise it was when Tomlinson said it. There is no exaggeration in the actors' performances, no studio audience to project to, and the banter moves to the rhythms of the fly-on-the-wall documentary rather than the sitcom. The dialogue is extraordinary because, for all its humour, it sounds so ordinary.

Apart from flies-on-walls, the past British TV shows which were nearest in tone to *The Royle Family* were by Mike Leigh, Steve Coogan and Victoria Wood. And in distilling comedy from conversations we have all had, it may be the sitcom Tony Hancock dreamed of making. Ironically, though, *The Royle Family*'s blue-collar naturalism finds its closest relation in the new wave of American cartoons: *King of the Hill*, foremost, but also *Beavis and Butt-Head*, if only because its protagonists are hypnotized by the television.

It's an old truism that people on TV never watch enough TV, but the Royles do little else. 'He's everywhere, him,' grumbles Jim when Chris Evans comes on. 'He's like shit in a field.' (Tomorrow's episode slips up, though, in putting David Attenborough on the box. When TV characters do watch TV, how come it's always wildlife programmes?)

Another truism is that there are too many middle-class sitcoms set in living-rooms, so Aherne and co must have relished setting *The Royle Family* in a living room that Terry and June wouldn't have recognized: one so cramped that Denise has to squeeze between the arm chair and the couch when she wants to go into the kitchen. We're not used to seeing such families on television. To be more accurate, we're not used to seeing them unless they're being ground down by joblessness, drug addiction, domestic violence and bedwetting.

The Royle Family has more affection for its characters: you don't need a crisis to make a comedy drama. Twinges of disgruntlement tighten their faces, but the Royles are fundamentally closeknit and warm – unlike, perhaps, the Royals. What we have here is a genuinely original sitcom, and if the quality keeps up, it will be a happy and glorious one. *The Royle Family* rules.

Sunday Independent, 20 September 1998

Class of '98
Charlotte Raven

It looked like it was going to be brilliant. A sitcom with working-class characters concerned with the rhythms of everyday life. *The Royle Family*'s unique selling point was its attempt to see its characters as people rather than issues ... the Royles pore over a catalogue, talk about money-off coupons, eat chips, buy some knock off gear ... Apart from anything else, the whole thing seems so old-fashioned.

The Royles are trapped in their class. None of them are given real characters. They have ended up simply as ciphers in a script which is both nostalgic for an idea of working-classness that was never really true and perversely fetishistic about the details. Perhaps it is only now – when fewer people than ever would define themselves as working-class, when it is no longer an identity so much as a series of signs – that a curious anachronism like The Royles could be produced. It feels almost like a museum in which aspects of working-class life have been collected, not disrespectfully, but somehow with a view to closing a chapter.

As a piece of semi-realist drama, *The Royle Family* doesn't stand up ... The script is so pleased with the word ['arse'] that it throws it in wherever possible, in defiance both of taste and the diminishing demands of veracity. For, as we know, in most 'respectable' working-class families, 'language' would be prohibited, for all the right reasons, of course.

The Royles doesn't care about this, keener as it is to please the viewer who has never heard 'arse' used in *Seinfeld*, so presumes it to be just another of those 'true to life' little details for which Caroline Aherne and her team have become so unjustly renowned.

Guardian G2, 17 September 1998

Manchester's benighted
Brian Viner

. . . All of which brings me to *The Royle Family*, a six-part comedy drama which dares to go further than any television series I can remember in replicating the comedy of real life. This means no orchestrated laughter from a studio audience, no plot, hardly any action and very few jokes, but quite a lot of nose-picking.

Unlike life, *The Royle Family* has a script, but as in life the dialogue seems improvized, while containing some cracking one-liners: ''E changes 'is clothes less than Noddy' was an irresistible piece of imagery which reminded me again of my wife's aunt, who once complained that the swimming pool in her Majorca hotel was not only too small but surrounded by high white walls, 'like a postage stamp in t'middle of a squash court'.

The setting for *The Royle Family* is the front room, occasionally extending to the kitchen, of a council flat in Greater Manchester. It's probably not far from the fictional suburb of Weatherfield, although *Coronation Street* offers a heightened version of reality, in which domestic crises abound and nobody ever watches telly or goes to the toilet. In *The Royle Family*, a domestic crisis means a heftier-than-usual phone bill, they watch telly constantly, and the toilet looms large.

It is said that the American sitcom *Seinfeld* is about nothing, yet it is of labyrinthine complexity alongside *The Royle Family*. The story, such as it is, has hairdresser Denise Royle (Caroline Aherne) preparing to marry mobile disco owner Dave Best (Craig Cash). Aherne and Cash – who also wrote *The Royle*

Family, with their regular collaborator Henry Normal – are better-known as Mrs Merton and her son Malcolm.

Similarly, Ricky Tomlinson and Sue Johnston, who play Denise's parents Jim and Barbara, were once united as *Brookside*'s Bobby and Sheila Grant. This goes some way to explain why they all act as though they've known each other for years – they have – although newcomer Ralf Little is just as natural as Denise's put-upon younger brother Antony.

With a lesser cast, *The Royle Family* might not have worked. As it is, it works triumphantly. It is unfair to single anyone out for particular praise, although I should say that Tomlinson does nothing to change my opinion, expressed before in this column, that he is our finest screen actor and a national treasure. He'd have been knighted by now if he looked and sounded more like a matinee idol and less like a garden gnome from Bootle. In fact, I'll go further and say that Tomlinson is twice the actor Kenneth Branagh is . . .

Mail on Sunday, 20 September 1998

Best comedy

There are no jokes and nothing much happens – but this is still the funniest thing on TV by a street. Admirably underplayed by Caroline Aherne, Sue Johnston, Ricky Tomlinson and Craig Cash, joined tonight by Liz Smith as Nana (it being Sunday afternoon), *The Royle Family* turns the mind-numbingly banal into classic comedy.

TV Quick, 23 September 1998

Pick of the night

Wind-breakingly funny new comedy, shot as if it were a fly-on-the-wall chronicle of an 'average' working-class family. Imagine if you will the Battersbys of *Coronation Street* beamed up (or down) into a Mike Leigh council-estate drama. It is scripted by the *Mrs Merton* team: Caroline Aherne, Craig Cash and Henry Normal. Indeed, Aherne appears in the show as daughter

Denise. This could have been a risky indulgence given Aherne's ability to dominate the screen, but the other characters are strong enough to ensure that the show remains an ensemble piece. Ricky Tomlinson and Sue Johnston (formerly Bobby and Sheila Grant in *Brookside*) are Dad and Mam, Craig Cash is Denise's fiancé Dave and Geoffrey Hughes (once Eddie Yeats in *Coronation Street*) is local entrepreneur Twiggy. Awesomely realistic performances all round, but Jessica Stevenson, as next door neighbour Cheryl, deserves special praise.

Evening Standard, 14 September 1998

The Royle Family

Another deliciously observed slice of life from Caroline Aherne and friends. Yet again, the subject under discussion, over a gourmet supper of pork chops, chips, beans and tea, is Denise's approaching wedding – with Jim grumbling about having to foot the entire bill because the groom's father has been on disability benefit for 12 years. 'But he's got a bone disease,' exclaims Denise. 'Yeah, and it's called bone-idleness,' retorts Jim. Brilliant.

Telegraph, 21 September 1998

Laugh? It was just like home
Flic Everett

Caroline Aherne, aka Mrs Merton, starred in a new TV comedy the other night, *The Royle Family*. I watched it with my boyfriend, and, both of us being from the north, we were doubled up with laughter after roughly 20 seconds, as the best observed living room scene I've ever witnesses opened up. Wittering mum, grumpy dad, irritable grown-up children. It was everyone's experience of a certain type of family, even if it wasn't your own family. And it was riveting and hilarious.

Next day, I read the reviews in the national papers to see if they'd enjoyed it as much as we did. Nope.

It was almost universally criticized for being unfunny, inexplicable and boring. Then it occurred to me that most TV critics are southerners, and can't possibly grasp the uniquely sarcastic griping that many northern families solely communicate in.

The fools. They don't know what they're missing.

Manchester Evening News, 17 September 1999

Caroline's Royle flush

I didn't mention Caroline Ahern's new comedy last week because I didn't want to judge it on one episode.

And because I forgot.

But I must mention it now – because it really is a gem.

The series, entitled *The Royle Family*, does take some getting used to.

There's no studio audience, no real plot and nothing you could strictly call a joke.

In fact, mostly the family just sit watching telly.

What holds it together – and sets it apart – is the gritty, witty dialogue. Exchanges such as:

'Dad, stop fiddling with yerself!'

'I'm not fiddling with meself. I paid a quid for these underpants and I've got 50 pence worth stuck up me arse.'

Don't be surprised to see Caroline and co collecting an award for this series at the next BAFTA ceremony.

She'll be the one swigging Tizer.

Daily Star, 25 September 1999

Acknowledgements

We would like to thank our brilliant cast:

Geoffrey Hughes, Sue Johnston, Doreen Keogh, Ralf Little, Peter Martin, Jessica Stevenson and Ricky Tomlinson.

And crew:

Chris Atkinson, David Boyle, Richard Brierley, Chris Clarkson, C Copple, Paul Copple, Tony Cranstoun, Alistair Davidson, Dick Dodd, Graham Etchells, Jill Farrimond, Sam Ferguson, M Fisher, Dorothy Friend, Elena Gabrilatsou, Lynne Gibson, Andy Harries, Jeremy Hiles, Ed Hoyle, Ann Humphreys, Chris Hutchinson, Keith Jones, Cal Lavelle, Susy Liddell, Ken Mair, Graham Meetho, Dominique Molloy, Pete Moran, Carmel Morgan, Jane Morris, Peter O'Rourke, Sharon Perks, Alan Scholes, Mike Sergeant, Lynne Todd, John Welsh, June West, Glenn Wilhide, Chris Wilkinson.

We would also like to thank the following:

Lucy Ansbro, BBC2, Kathy Burke, Mark Gorton, Granada Television, Michael Jackson, Peter Kessler, Jimmy McGovern, Phil McIntyre, Pati Marr, Carmel Morgan, Jan Murphy, Paul Roberts, Simon Shaps, Norma Smith, Matt Squire, Mark Thompson, Brian Viner, John Whiston, Andrea Wonfor – and all at Creation Records.